Successful Boxing

The Ultimate Training Manual

Successful Boxing

The Ultimate Training Manual

Andy Dumas & Jamie Dumas

THE CROWOOD PRESS

First published in 2013 by
The Crowood Press Ltd
Ramsbury, Marlborough
Wiltshire SN8 2HR

www.crowood.com

This impression 2017

British Library Cataloguing-in-Publication Data
A catalogue record for this book is available from the British Library.

ISBN 978 1 84797 462 4

Dedication
Dedicated to our parents, Eve and Cliff Dumas Sr, and Joyce and Joseph Lipton

Acknowledgements
Our thanks go to the great Sergio Martinez, Juan Manuel Márquez, Saúl Álvarez, Julio César Chávez Jr, Jose Sulaiman and Mauricio Sulaiman of the World Boxing Council (WBC); Jill Diamond, WBC Female Championship Committee; Jeanie Kahnke of the Muhammad Ali Center; Brian DeMaris of Balazs Boxing; Russ Anber, Julia Smith and everyone at Rival Boxing; Cleto Reyes; Headsweats, Champion Boxing Club Brampton, Ontario; David Hart, John Poirier, Otis Sutherland, Donovan Irving and the 'gang' at Huron Park Boxing.

Photo credits
Live action boxing photographs by Naoki Fakuda (www.naopix.com)
Instructional photographs by Andy Dumas, Jamie Dumas (www.andydumas.ca) and Troy Moth (www.troymoth.com)

Disclaimer
Please note that the authors and the publisher of this book, and those others who have contributed to it, are not responsible in any manner whatsoever for any damage or injury of any kind that may result from practising, or applying, the principles, ideas, techniques and/ or following the instructions/information described in this publication. Since the physical activities described in this book may be too strenuous in nature for some readers to engage in safely, it is essential that a doctor be consulted before participating.

Also by Andy Dumas and Jamie Dumas, *The One-Two Punch Boxing Workout*, and *Knockout Fitness.*

Typeset by Bookcraft, Stroud, Gloucestershire
Printed and bound by CPI Group (UK) Ltd, Croydon, CR0 4YY

CONTENTS

FOREWORD

I am a warrior. Fighting is what I do.

Being a fighter has always been a large part of my life. I believe that pushing myself to the limit and being the best I can be, has led me to success. I face the toughest and most talented fighters in the world. Each and every time I step into the ring I meet the challenge with determination and the knowledge that I am physically and mentally prepared.

For the world, a boxing match is a primal sporting event, a show, entertainment. For a boxer, each fight has the potential to be an important turning point in his life.

Countless hours of training and conditioning, throwing punches on the heavy bag and sparring in the ring are spent preparing for competition. *Successful Boxing* breaks down the punches, training routines, and conditioning into specific and precise tips to provide a basis to develop and improve your performance. This book is a complete resource of the punches, offensive and defensive moves, footwork, fitness, agility and strategic planning needed to become a successful boxer.

It selects the best of 'old-school' training and incorporates it with the latest scientific and technical information and can easily be referenced during your training sessions.

Successful Boxing provides insight and inspiration to attain your personal best.

Juan Manuel Márquez

Juan Manuel Márquez has won seven world titles in four different weight classes. Currently, Márquez is the WBO Lightweight World Champion. He is also currently rated by The Ring *magazine as the number six pound-for-pound boxer in the world. He is considered by many to be one of the greatest Mexican boxers of all time.*

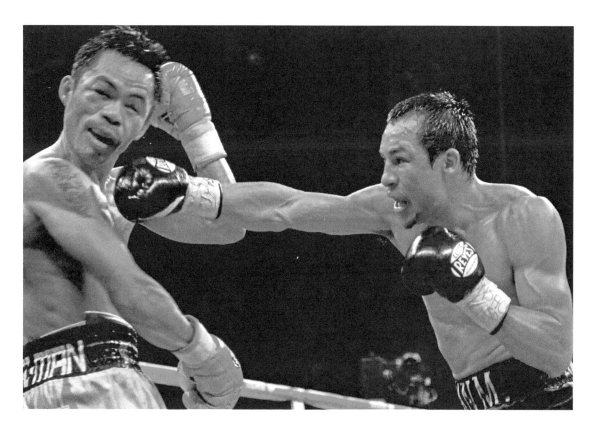

Márquez vs Pacquiao.

PREFACE

What is the definition of success? For us, success is the peace of mind attained when we have done everything possible to become our very best. Every day we are faced with the choices that ultimately decide whether we succeed. We make the choice to put our heart and soul into everything that we do. A champion takes pleasure in the process of training and creating a strong, lean, healthy body so that every movement is executed with perfection. The will to prepare mentally and physically makes all the difference.

Successful Boxing is the ultimate training book on boxing. This indispensable resource for boxers shares tips and suggestions on how to improve skills and maximize performance. With inspiration and advice from World Champions Sergio Martinez, Saúl Álvarez and Julio César Chávez Jr, and a Foreword by legendary World Champion Juan Manuel Márquez,

Andy Dumas.

Jamie Dumas.

Successful Boxing is an excellent alternative to receiving private sessions with a coach. The tips and training methods shown in the book allow you to master the individual nuances of boxing which will give you the winning edge.

Over the years we have been fortunate enough to spend time with some of the greatest names in boxing: Alexis Arguello, Roberto Duran, Sugar Ray Leonard, Evander Holyfield, Julio César Chávez, Lennox Lewis, Ken Norton, Floyd Mayweather Jr, Ricky Hatton, Larry Holmes, Marvelous Marvin Hagler, Erik Morales, Tommy Hearns, and the legendary trainer Angelo Dundee.

Over the past few years (2007–12), Andy has been involved with projects at the Ali Center in Louisville, Kentucky, and has had several opportunities to spend time with his idol, Muhammad Ali. For decades Ali has inspired millions around the world to be their best, to work hard and be dedicated. We hope this book motivates you to get in the finest physical condition possible, and in some small way inspires you to be your very best.

Whether you are new to the sport or a serious competitor, this book will help you reach the next level of skill development. *Successful Boxing* is the perfect companion for any student of the 'sweet science'.

Andy Dumas and Jamie Dumas

Andy with Muhammad Ali.

CHAPTER I

WINNING SPIRIT

Successful boxers have the intrinsic desire to win. They possess the dedication and determined commitment necessary to be victorious. In most fights, there comes a point when both fighters are exhausted. This is a defining moment and the boxer who decides to put forth that extra effort is probably going to win. This extra effort is the 'winning spirit'. Boxers must learn to give their best effort no matter what the situation and we believe that all training should be designed to teach the winning spirit.

Champion Nonito Donaire.

In boxing it is unrealistic to believe that athletes will never experience losing. It hurts to lose, but it gives you the chance to learn and improve and to make the changes necessary to avoid repeating the same mistakes. Boxers need to develop the resilience and mental toughness to bounce back from disappointment. Facing a tough opponent can create a drive and determination to work harder. Great boxers thrive in competitive situations, and a good opponent will bring out the best in you.

Boxing is one of the most challenging activities that you will ever do. It teaches you to rely on yourself, building self-confidence and character. You learn to place worth on advice from others, to respect your own skill level and the skill level of your opponents. Boxing is challenging and has many rewards, including the development of athleticism, sportsmanship, physical and mental conditioning, and self-worth.

The Coach Makes the Gym

The most important attribute of a coach is the ability to communicate his boxing knowledge and to help his boxer reach his full potential in a safe training environment. Look for a coach/trainer who knows the game inside out and exhibits a true passion for the sport. Canadian boxing coach Russ Anber states:

> To me there is no such thing as a good boxing club, there are only good coaches. You can take the best coaches, put them in a garage with a ring and a couple of heavy bags, and produce good fighters. To me the coach makes the gym.

Coaches make the gym.

Look for a coach who is certified with one of the national boxing associations. There are generally five different levels of certification that a boxing coach/ trainer may achieve. Level one certification qualifies a trainer to work at a local boxing gym. A boxing trainer with level one certification typically works with beginning amateur boxers, or people who just wish to improve their physical fitness through boxing classes. Subsequent certification levels require a boxing trainer to gain extensive practical experience and demonstrate a strong understanding of boxing theory. Level five certified boxing trainers are qualified to work with Olympic-level boxers and full-time professional boxers.

Look for a certified coach.

Russ Anber insists that:

The most important quality in a coach is the ability to teach. I would rather have a guy with average knowledge, but is an excellent teacher. Knowledge will come to him. There are so many people that have an infinite amount of knowledge but have no teaching skills. They are not able to express their message and explain to someone in a way they can understand it. To me the teacher is the most important thing.

Watch a coach working with other boxers. Observe the interaction between the coach and the boxer. Does the coach give clear, direct and consistent instructions to the boxer? Does he show patience and motivate his boxer without being demeaning or overcritical? Does the boxer appear to understand the directions from the coach and then successfully follow the instructions? A good coach will identify your strengths and weaknesses, bring out the best in you and put you on a training schedule specific to your skill level.

Your initial training sessions and workouts at the boxing gym will give you insight into your boxing trainer's ability. A quality trainer will not risk injury when they know you have not yet gained the capabilities or conditioning. If you are being thrown into sparring almost immediately, you should consider finding yourself a different boxing trainer.

Make sure that you find a boxing trainer who, at the start, takes the time to figure out the type of fighter you are, and then, perhaps weeks or even months later, will start you off with some light gym sparring with other boxers of a similar ability and in the same weight class. He will also ensure that the sparring is controlled and that an experienced boxer helps a less experienced boxer rather than taking advantage of their inexperience. Good trainers need

A good coach will bring out the best in you.

Manny Pacquiao.

to keep their boxer motivated. They must also know when the boxer has had enough physically, and has reached their limit mentally.

> I live by the axiom that learning and hard work are not the enemy of fun. And I believe that. Why can't you learn to develop skills and have fun in the process? Learn to do it well, work hard, learn skills and be better than you were when you walked into the gym and still enjoy your time there.
>
> *Russ Anber*

Look for a boxing club with a variety of equipment: a ring, heavy bags, double-end bags and speed bags, large mirrors for shadowboxing, focus mitts, boxing gloves and water available. Ensure the club is open at times that are convenient for your training schedule.

Know what you are looking for in a club and a trainer. An experienced trainer and positive gym environment should produce athletes that are dedicated, motivated and hard-working.

Positive attitude and perseverance are a personal choice. To succeed at any sport, an individual must internalize certain qualities. A successful boxer will show the following ten qualities:

1 self-respect
2 a desire to learn and improve
3 the will to win
4 self-discipline
5 self-control
6 competitive perseverance
7 hard work and will-power to achieve goals
8 the ability to focus and perform under pressure
9 the resilience and perseverance to rebound from defeat
10 demonstration of sportsmanship and fair play.

BEING A CHAMPION

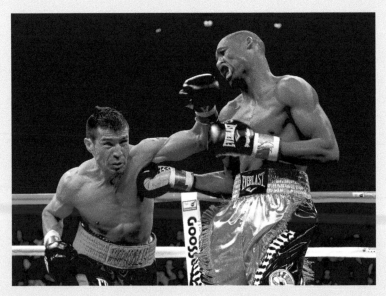

Martinez lands a knockout punch.

Throughout its long history the 'sweet science' has always been a test of physical fitness and physical prowess. Boxing started as a means of resolving disagreements, and a victorious fighter displaying bravery, strength and courage was held in high regard in his community. These characteristics still remain, but boxing has developed into more of a contest of skill, talent and dedication. Boxing had a primitive beginning, with few or no rules, and has advanced into an intricate physical science of fighting.

Boxing is very noble and very clean. It is a healthy sport when well executed. It is important to have daily motivation, the will to succeed, and perseverance in your work. Talent may be important, but without the other three you can't truly achieve greatness. I visualize fights with my opponents knowing that I will win in every aspect. It motivates me every day to work harder.

When I train, I strive to be my best, to focus, watch, listen and learn. I am not satisfied with 'good enough'. I am the person you'll see training every day when everyone else has left the gym. Every time I compete, I try harder to improve on my last performance and give my very best effort, to go the distance and to never quit. These things are the fundamental challenges. They are what make me alive by any definition that I know.

In every battle, there is an instant that separates victory from defeat. A true champion recognizes and seizes that moment by giving an effort so passionate and so intense that it could only come from deep down in his heart. To win, you must have passion for the sport, determination and complete faith in yourself. The thing that distinguishes great athletes from everyone else is the ability to excel in times of great stress, urgency and pressure. I never want an easy fight. I want to fight the best. Being a champion is about facing, and beating, the best.

Love what you do, share that passion with others and always stay humble.

Sergio 'Maravilla' Martinez

Sergio Martinez is the current World Middleweight Champion, and the current WBC World Middleweight title holder; he is also the former WBC Super Welterweight Champion. The Ring magazine currently ranks Martinez as the number three pound-for-pound boxer in the world.

CHAPTER 2

BASICS OF THE 'SWEET SCIENCE'

Boxing Stance

All moves in boxing start from the strong foundation of a balanced boxing stance that allows you to shift easily from defensive to offensive moves. The balanced boxing stance facilitates stability and mobility when throwing a wide assortment of punches and combinations. From this stance you can attack or defend without an advanced warning to your opponent.

Floyd Mayweather Jr.

Most boxers adopt the orthodox or classic boxing stance, with the left foot forward and leading with the left jab. Generally this is the preferred stance if your dominant hand is your right hand.

'Southpaw' is a boxing term that designates the stance where the boxer has his right hand and right foot forward, leading with a right jab. Southpaw is the normal stance if your dominant hand is your left hand.

Classic Stance

The Legs and Feet

The legs and feet are the most important element of an effective boxing stance. If the feet are not in the correct position you will not be able to elude punches or throw punches correctly. For the orthodox or classic boxer (right-hand dominant), stand with the feet shoulder-width apart and step forward with the left foot. The front or lead foot points toward your opponent. The back or trail foot is behind and slightly to the side. Ensure that the trail foot is not directly behind the front foot. Your feet should be in a three-quarter stance. This is the starting foot position for an orthodox boxer.

Balance your body weight equally between both legs, staying on the balls of the feet, with the back heel raised slightly. Remaining on the ball of your back foot gives you more mobility and the raised heel allows you to respond and move more easily and pivot or rotate when you throw punches with your dominant hand. Ensure that the weight is distributed evenly between both legs, with perhaps a little more weight on the rear foot, allowing for

Classic boxing stance.

Southpaw stance – Martinez waiting for the bell.

quick movements forward, backward and side-to-side. Slightly bend the knees to lower your centre of gravity, giving a solid base from which to execute your punches. If your legs are too close together you will be off-balance and unable to move and throw effectively. If your legs are too far apart, your response time will be hindered. The best boxing stance is one that allows you to move easily in any direction and provides a strong solid base for developing perfect synchronization of the arms, the body and leg movements. From a balanced boxing stance you can effectively move, attack and defend.

For southpaws (left-hand dominant), reverse the feet. The right foot is the lead foot and the left foot is the trailing foot.

Body Orientation

You want to minimize the target area that you present to your opponent. Stand with your body angled and partially sideways, aligning the front shoulder, hip and front foot to make your body less exposed and reducing the size of the target. The lead shoulder and lead arm are closer to your opponent, which is why the jab should be the most frequently thrown punch. The angled body position also enables you to generate the torque and speed needed to produce a powerful punch with your rear/dominant hand. Protect your body by holding the core muscles tight and rounding the shoulders slightly forward in a relaxed position. The power in your punch is generated from a strong centred core and strong balanced legs.

The Arms and Fists

The fist and arm positioning is determined by your offensive and defensive requirements during a fight. Your arms and fists provide defensive protection against your opponent's blows. The hands and arms should always be in the on-guard position, unless you are delivering punches or defending against punches. Always bring the fists back to the on-guard position after throwing a punch. The hands are held high to protect the head and can be used to block or parry punches. The arms are held close to the sides of the body and bent at the elbows, protecting the rib cage and solar plexus. The position of the elbows can be adjusted to defend against body punches.

The left fist is turned slightly inward and held close to the chin. The right fist is held just above the right shoulder. Make a fist by loosely closing the fingers in toward the palm and fold the thumb on the outside of the fingers. Orthodox boxers keep the right fist close to the chin, slightly higher than the left fist. The left hand is high enough to cover your chin but low enough to allow you to see over it. All punches are thrown from this position (reverse for southpaws).

Sometimes imitating your favourite fighter can get you into trouble. The great Muhammad Ali, who often held his arms down at his sides, had tremendous speed and agility to be able to move away from his opponent. Sergio Martinez, Manny Pacquiao and Floyd Mayweather Jr also have the ability to keep clear of punches from unorthodox positions. These elite fighters developed these skills after years and years of training. Most boxers do not have this ability. Do not get caught. Always keep your fists up.

The Head and Neck

With the neck and shoulders relaxed, keep your eyes in the direction of your opponent. Hold the head slightly down with the chin tucked in toward the chest to reduce the chance of getting caught with a head shot. With the chin tucked in the throat is protected and makes your jaw less of a target. The chin is protected by the right fist and left shoulder (left fist and right shoulder for southpaws). You never want your chin exposed as it leaves you vulnerable to a knockout blow.

Check Your Classic Boxing Stance

- Legs and feet in balanced position.
- Body stays relaxed.
- Front/lead foot points toward your opponent.
- Back/trail foot is behind and slightly to the side, but not directly behind the front foot.
- Body weight balanced equally between both legs, staying on the balls of the feet, and back heel raised slightly.
- Slight bend at the knees to lower your centre of gravity.
- Body core muscles held tight.
- Body angled to your opponent, aligning the front shoulder, hip and front foot.
- Arms held by the sides of the body and bent at the elbows to protect the rib cage.
- Fingers closed loosely and thumb folded to the outside of the fingers.
- Fists turned in slightly and held high in the on-guard position.

The following are some common mistakes encountered by boxers. Be aware of these errors and use the training tips to correct them.

COMMON ERRORS AND QUICK FIXES

Error: Too tense through the shoulder and neck region.

Quick fix: Relax the muscles of the shoulders and neck. Keep your chin tucked in toward the chest. The most effective punches come from a relaxed position.

Error: The trail foot is directly behind the lead foot.

Quick fix: To stay balanced and ready to move the lead foot points toward your opponent and the trail foot is behind and slightly to the side of the lead foot.

Error: Knees are too straight.

Quick fix: Bend the knees slightly to allow for a faster side-to-side, front-to-back, and up-and-down movement and better response time.

The Execution of a Punch

The correct execution of a single punch requires repetition after repetition until you have mastered the skill. Punching imagery, focus and a positive attitude will assist in the progression of this skill, allowing for a stronger and better executed punch. Hours and hours of training, quick thinking, explosive power and elite physical conditioning create great punch combinations, but it all starts with a single punch.

In order for punches to be correctly and effectively executed the body must stay relaxed and breathing must be constant and controlled. Breathe naturally and exhale as you throw your punches. This will result in the abdominal muscles tightening and may assist in absorbing a body punch.

The Left Jab

The jab is the most important and frequently thrown punch in your arsenal. It can be used as an offensive and defensive weapon. It creates openings for more powerful punches and keeps your opponent at a safe distance. A crisp jab is the most effective weapon in boxing, and during any given round jabs should be thrown almost continually. Entire fights can be controlled with a series of effective jabs.

To throw a jab, fire your left hand in a straight line toward your target. Your fist stays relaxed and tightens just before impact of the knuckles of the pointer finger and middle finger. Snap your jabs quickly without hyper-extending your arm at the elbow joint, and during the last third of the punch distance rotate the forearm so the knuckles are face down. As you launch the jab, push off the ball of the back foot slightly and move the front foot forward. This will give you additional power behind the punch. The fastest and most effective punches travel in a straight line and return along the same path.

With this left jab arm extended you are more vulnerable to counterpunches. Therefore the fist must immediately return straight back to the on-guard position to protect your head. Also, keep the non-punching hand close to the chin, and the elbow by the side of the body to protect the torso and ribs.

Left jab.

COMMON ERRORS AND QUICK FIXES

Error: Before launching a punch, the fist is either dropped slightly or pulled back.

Quick fix: The old-school term for when you drop or pull back your punch is 'telegraphing'. This will tip off your opponent. Practice in front of the mirror to make sure your punches are launched straight from the on-guard position.

Error: Dropping hands after throwing a punch.

Quick fix: This is a lazy habit and difficult to break. This leaves you vulnerable to counterpunches. Get in the routine of throwing your punches straight out and straight back.

Error: Jab is slow and sloppy.

Quick fix: Snap the jab, shifting your weight forward and line up your body behind the punch.

As the most frequently thrown punch, the jab can be thrown effectively from any position while moving.

The Straight Right/Right Cross

The straight right can be an extremely powerful punch and is often referred to as the 'knock-out' punch. The power of this punch is the result of the torque produced by the turning of the shoulders, driving off the ball of the trail foot, and the simultaneous rotation of the hips. The right should be thrown with serious intent, but not wild. There is a danger of throwing this punch wild and over-extending, causing you to become off-balance. Keep the core abdominal muscles tight in order to keep your balance centred. There is also a tendency to lunge forward with your body, leaving you open and vulnerable.

Since the straight right has further to travel to the target it has to be thrown extremely quickly and accurately. The power of the right hand can be used to force an opponent that gets too close to back off. Your dominant hand is your more powerful, stronger hand. This is the main reason your dominant hand should be in the back.

From the on-guard position launch the right arm away from the body as you rotate the right hip forward and pivot on the ball of the back foot. As with the jab, rotate the forearm during the last third of the punch distance so the knuckles are face down.

Maintain your guard with your left hand to protect your chin. Ensure you do not pull the arm or lift the elbow before throwing the punch. This is called 'telegraphing' a punch and will tip off your opponent to the oncoming punch. When contact is made, the right arm is almost fully extended, the hips square to the target and the chin down. Because it takes more time to throw the straight right, you are more easily open to counterpunches. Quickly return to the protective on-guard position, preparing for the next punch.

The right cross, similar to a straight right, is a counterpunch thrown when slipping a left jab. It is thrown

Straight right.

COMMON ERRORS AND QUICK FIXES

Error: The trail foot lifts off the floor when launching the straight right, reducing its effectiveness and causing you to be off-balance.

Quick fix: The foot must remain in contact with the ground. As you launch the punch, pivot and drive off the ball of the trail foot. Execute the move slowly and check in a mirror for correct execution.

Error: Dropping your left fist as you launch your straight right.

Quick fix: A lowered left guard leaves you open to a counterpunch. Any movement that tips off your opponent that a punch is coming should be avoided. Keep the left fist high and even let the glove touch the left side of the head as a reminder.

across the left jab with a slight arc, unlike the straight right, which is thrown in a straight line. Timing of the right crossover the left jab is crucial as you are vulnerable to a counterpunch, such as a left hook.

The Left Hook

The left hook can be a tremendously powerful punch when thrown properly. It is most effective when executed at close range outside your opponent's range of vision and can easily catch your opponent off-guard. All-time great boxing trainer Angelo Dundee believed that a strong left hook, because of its proximity to the opponent, can consistently do more damage than a right cross.

Left hook.

Start in the classic boxing stance, with the core held tight, the body weight centred evenly through both legs and knees slightly bent. Pivot on the ball of the front foot, quickly rotating the arm, shoulder, body and hips in one movement. The transfer of the force generated from the front foot pivot and rotation of the body gives the hooking arm its power. The left elbow is raised away from the side of the body with the underside of the arm parallel to the floor. It is bent at a 90-degree angle. The position of the fist can be parallel to the ground or facing your opponent. After the punch is thrown, return to the on-guard position.

You must be in close range to your opponent for the hook to be effective. The main advantage of the hook is its surprise element. The hook is a more deceptive punch as it moves approximately one third of the distance of a straight right. Keep your chin tucked in, with the right fist in the protective position, ready to block a potential counterpunch.

Hooks can be thrown effectively to your opponent's body or head. Do not drop your hand to throw a hook to the body; rather bend the knees to lower your body. As with a hook to the head, throw the punch in a lateral arc level with and across the shoulder.

The right hook comes from the rear hand and off the trail foot. The arm position is similar to the left

---

COMMON ERRORS AND QUICK FIXES

Error: The left hand does not return to the on-guard position after throwing the hook. The chin is left unprotected.

Quick fix: After the punch makes contact, immediately bring the fist back up into the on-guard position.

Error: The body does not turn with the punch as a unit, reducing the effectiveness and power of the punch. The arm moves without the rotation through the body.

Quick fix: Practise keeping the body and punch arm synchronized, with the elbow, hip and knee moving in one piece, while pivoting on the ball of the lead foot.

hook, but the shoulder and arm must move further for the fist to make contact. This makes it a slower punch and more easily detected and leaves your right side open to a counterpunch. Only use a right hook when fighting at close range.

The Uppercut

Boxers are taught to fight from a distance, keeping their opponent on the end of their punches. Because it is a short-range punch, the uppercut is often ignored or under-utilized. Throwing uppercuts can be risky as you are left open to counterpunches while you momentarily drop your guard to launch the punch. If you are close enough to land an uppercut, you are also close enough to get hit back with a power shot.

The uppercut can either be thrown to the body, affecting your opponent's balance and strength, or explode as a devastating punch to the chin. For the orthodox fighter the right uppercut is slightly more powerful, but this punch can be thrown effectively with either hand.

To throw the right uppercut, begin in the classic boxing stance with the right knee slightly bent. Dip the right shoulder down, lowering the body to the right side. While keeping the left fist high to protect the head, press into the ball of the front foot, rotating forward through the hips and launching your right fist toward the target. During delivery and follow through keep the right elbow bent at a right angle. The release of the fist is perfectly timed with the hip rotation and the pressing of the front foot into the floor. The uppercut should land on the target as the hips finish rotating and be timed to have maximum power on impact. Keep the punch tight and close to the body. Over-extending with wild punches and misses leaves you off-balance and vulnerable to counterpunches. Always pull the fist straight back to

Right uppercut.

COMMON ERRORS AND QUICK FIXES

Error: Winding up before launching the uppercut.

Quick fix: Winding up will clearly indicate to your opponent that a punch is coming. Keep the elbows close to the body, abdominal muscles held tight, and the shoulders rounded forward.

Error: Trying to land the uppercut from a distance.

Quick fix: You must be in close range to land an uppercut. Set up your uppercuts with straight punches first and move in to your target.

Error: Trying to throw the uppercut too hard.

Quick fix: Throwing punches too hard is often called 'loading up' and this will throw you off-balance. Obtain your classic boxing stance and use the transfer of your body weight to put more power behind the punch. Slow down the move until it feels natural and practise in front of the mirror. The mirror is your best friend when working on technique and checking your form.

your chin with a plan to throw another uppercut or stay in the on-guard position.

To throw the left uppercut, transfer your weight onto the ball of your left foot and deliver the punch with a bent arm held at a right angle. The hips rotate with the left knee slightly bent and the left shoulder lowered. Keep the hands up and the punch motion tight, using the upward torque force from the hips and legs to intensify the power on impact.

Successful boxers should always anticipate a few moves ahead. Possible follow-up punches for a right uppercut to the head could be a left hook. The left uppercut to the head can be followed with a straight right. Uppercuts thrown to the body may cause your opponent's body to fall slightly forward, creating an opening for you to land hooks or a right cross. Stay close to the target, so your opponent will not easily detect the punch and a counterpunch such as a straight right is prevented.

COMMON ERRORS AND QUICK FIXES

Error: Incorrect leg position with the body weight on the heels of your feet and the stance too narrow or too wide.

Quick fix: A stance that is too narrow or too wide will throw you off-balance and affect your timing. Stay on the balls of the feet, keeping the body weight forward and the feet about shoulder-width apart.

Error: Taking large, lunging steps as you move. This over-emphasized movement not only puts you off-balance, it also tips off your opponent.

Quick fix: Movement should be smooth in all directions, feet staying close to the floor. Practise moving forward, backward, side-to-side and on angles, taking smaller steps in a controlled motion.

Footwork and Movement

Well-balanced footwork is essential in the ring. Fast legs and the movement that they generate are the foundation for all boxing moves. Boxers must move and shift their weight back and forth to set up an attack, as well as to avoid getting hit. Movement should be calculated and help you achieve your goal.

Advancing movements begin with moving the lead foot first as you push off from the trail foot. Retreating movements are initiated by moving the trail foot first and then the lead foot follows. When moving to the left, move the left foot first and the right foot follows. When moving to the right, move the right foot first and the left foot follows.

Do not lunge toward or away from your opponent. Trying to cover too much ground by taking large steps will throw you off-balance. Focus on moving smoothly in all directions while maintaining your balance and think in terms of small, efficient moves. Remember to push off the feet instead of stepping with the feet. If you step, the heel of the foot will strike the floor first making movement and directional changes very difficult. Stay on the balls of the feet using your footwork to get in and out of

punch range.

The art of moving smoothly around the boxing ring must be well practised. Developing a natural fluidity to advancing, retreating and moving side-to-side must be mastered.

Feints and Slips

Adding slips and feints to your punching combinations will bring another dimension to your training.

Feints

Feints are utilized to make your opponent think you are going to do one thing but you do another. By using your eyes, fists, body and legs, feints will test your opponent's reaction and create openings for a counterpunch.

There are a few ways to use shoulder and arm feints to confuse your opponent. One of the safest ways to feint is to use the shoulders. Jerk your shoulder forward like you are going to throw a jab, but do not extend the arm. Observe your opponent's response. Simply appear to throw a punch in a specific direction, wait a split second and then execute

COMMON ERRORS AND QUICK FIXES

Error: Leaving your fist out of position after feinting.

Quick fix: Dropping your hands after feinting will leave you vulnerable to a counterpunch. You must either return the fist to the on-guard position or throw a punch.

Error: Over-exaggerating your feints.

Quick fix: There is no surprise factor if your opponent knows what is coming. Practise subtle feints in front of a mirror to make sure they are realistic.

the punch with intent. You can also feint a jab, pause and throw a punch with the other hand or you can just feint without throwing a punch and just move away. Always keep your opponent guessing.

Shadowboxing in front of a mirror is a good place to practise feinting. Set up head punches by feinting punches to the body and vice versa. Set up left-handed punches with a right feint and right-handed punches with a left feint.

Slips

Learning how to slip punches is not only an advanced boxing technique it is an essential defensive skill. Slipping is a manoeuvre used to evade an oncoming punch. An effective slip allows you to stay in range to throw punches of your own. Employ a side-to-side movement of the head and shoulders, fist in the on-guard position, and a slight bend at the waist and knees so the incoming punch 'slips' safely past you. Most importantly, do not lean back. Lean slightly sideways, keeping your opponent in view. After slipping prepare to throw a counterpunch.

ABOVE: Slip to the right.
BELOW: Slip to the left.

Ricky Hatton. Develop smooth, fluid combinations.

To slip a left jab, move the head and shoulders to the right, bending at the waist and knees. To slip a straight right, move the head and shoulders to the left remembering to keep the hands up.

Developing Effective Punch Combinations

Start by perfecting your punch form and throwing technique; speed and power will develop later. Practise putting punches together so that one punch easily flows into the next. If a punch or slip throws you off-balance slightly, your follow-up punch should get you back on-balance. For example, after a straight right is thrown your body is in the correct position to throw a left hook. After throwing the left hook the body returns to the balanced boxing stance ready for the next move.

Simply throwing a series of fast, sloppy punches will get you nowhere. If you are having trouble with your punch combinations, slow down, throw fewer punches and concentrate on proper execution. Your combinations should be designed to throw off your opponent. Practise throwing punches to the body area and then up to the head. Double up on your jabs or throw two hooks consecutively. Add feints

and slips and ensure your moves are unpredictable.

Work on specific combinations until the movement is fluid. Try adding different punches to your combinations to mix up your moves. Vary the tempo, speed and power of your punches. Throw a few fast, crisp jabs, then one at three-quarter speed and finish with a strong, fast, unexpected jab with your body weight behind it. Changing the tempo and speed of the punches will keep your opponent on the edge.

Shadowboxing

One of the main purposes of shadowboxing is to loosen up the body and warm up the muscles and joints. It prepares the body for the physical demands that lie ahead and, when the moves are executed correctly, also develops muscle memory. Each move is fluid and effortless. Executing proper technique when you are shadowboxing not only conditions the body and develops the mind, but teaches you to react effectively when you train on the bags and focus mitts, and when you spar.

In boxing, your opponent will always try to make you miss. The fact is you are going to miss more punches than you land. When you train on the heavy bag the power and the momentum of your punches are absorbed into the bag and therefore you are able to recover to your balanced stance quickly. When shadowboxing you are only throwing punches in the air and not actually making contact. This teaches the body to counteract the momentum generated by your punches, developing core strength, coordination and balance.

Practice your footwork first, moving around in all directions. Once again remember to keep the hands in the on-guard position using imagery to slip and move. Add some jabs to make the movement quick and smooth. Visualize your opponent in front of you and slip out of the way. Throw some more punches. Use your imagination as you practise attacking and defensive moves. Good balance and fast footwork are the key elements to build quickness and responsiveness.

If you are comfortable with single punches, start to add two- and three-punch combinations. Work on lateral movement, keep your feet moving and stay on your toes. Continue to vary the selection of your punches, adding slips and feints to your combinations. As with a real boxing round, you should shadowbox at a fast pace in three-minute rounds and train the body to recognize the length of a round. Always challenge yourself so you feel slightly out of breath, eager and ready for more rounds.

Visualize your opponent as you practise offensive and defensive moves.

Mirror training allows you to perfect your punches and footwork by seeing how you are performing. If a particular combination feels awkward or your hands are out of position it is more easily detected and

Saúl Álvarez. Add feints and slips to your punch combinations.

Perfect your punches in front a mirror.

corrected. Keep the movements and punches simple at first and always have a mental image of what you want to achieve. Focus on speed and not power. Find a comfortable rhythm and match smooth footwork with crisp, fast punches.

Some boxers like to challenge themselves, holding onto light hand weights (1–1.5kg; 2–3lb), when shadowboxing. This slightly increased weight of the hand weights helps to build muscle endurance in the arm and shoulder regions, and challenges you to keep your hands up. Shadowboxing with hand weights should only be done after thoroughly warming up. Special care needs to be taken when using the hand weights. Throw your punches only at sixty per cent intensity, keep a firm grasp on the weights and always ensure you are executing the punch correctly.

Work the following classic combinations into your shadowboxing routines.

COMMON ERRORS AND QUICK FIXES

Error: Clumsy footwork while throwing punches.

Quick fix: Smooth footwork and fast punches should go hand in hand. If you are having trouble putting both together, keep your hands up and practise your footwork without combinations. Gradually flick some jabs as you move around and then the combinations will start to flow.

Error: Not moving while throwing punches.

Quick fix: Would you just stand there if you had a real, live opponent in front of you? You must realistically visualize your opponent and constantly move when shadowboxing. Feint, slip, move and throw plenty of punches.

Classic Combinations

- Double and triple jabs.
- Left jab to the body–left jab to the head.
- The one-two (left jab followed by a straight right).
- One-two hook (left jab, straight right, left hook).
- Right–left–right (right lead followed by a left hook, finish with a quick right).
- Left jab–left hook–straight right–left hook.
- Left jab–right uppercut–left hook.
- One-two–uppercut (left jab, straight right, left uppercut).

- Double jab–straight right (two quick left jabs followed by a straight right).
- One-two to the body–one-two to the head (left jab, straight right to the body: left jab straight right to the head).

Concentrate on proper punch execution. Place your best or favourite punch at the end of a sequence. Vary the selection. Order the punches so that you will finish on-balance and in the classic boxing stance, ready to shift quickly into the next move. By shadowboxing against an imaginary opponent, effective tactical skills can be developed.

Stay busy. Throw 'punches in bunches'.

CHAPTER 3

PUNCH-BAG WORKOUTS

Punch-bag workouts provide high intensity training sessions. The boxer completes repeated series of combination punches, develops coordination skills, timing and endurance, and also gains the confidence to be able to react under pressure.

Hitting the heavy bag gives you the opportunity to feel the strength, power and speed from your punches. Working the speed bag challenges your coordination skills and develops quickness. Punching the double-end bag develops agility and reaction time.

El Canelo works the heavy bag.

Protecting Your Hands

Hand Wraps

There are dozens of different techniques for hand wrapping. Each becomes individualistic and ritualistic to the boxer. Hand wraps protect the small bones of the hands, give support to the wrists and prevent abrasions to the knuckles. Training without hand wraps leads to a greater risk of short-term and long-term injuries, and discomfort.

Make sure the tension of the wrap is even on the hands and feels snug but not too tight. Use hand wraps that are 400–450cm (160–180in) long with some give to them (such as a Mexican hand wrap with Lycra).

How to wrap your hands

Step 1 Start by keeping your fingers spread apart, hands open and relaxed. Take the loop of the wrap and place it over the thumb. Ensure the wrap falls over to the front part of the wrist and hand.

Step 2 Wrap around the wrist once or twice in the direction away from the body and once around the thumb.

Step 3 Keeping the fingers spread apart, take the wrap around the knuckles three to four times. Make a fist to check that the tension of the wrap is not too tight. Ensure that the wrap is flat against the skin, with a slight overlap.

Step 4 Take the wrap to the base of the thumb. Loop the wrap three times between the fingers using the thumb as the anchor. Start with the wrap going over the back of the hand and then between the small finger and ring finger, back to the base of the thumb again, over the back side of the hand and then wrap between the ring finger and the long finger. Repeat for the last finger, finishing at the wrist.

Step 5 Take the wrap around the knuckles a few more times. Keep the wrap taut, making a fist to ensure a snug, but not too tight fit.

Step 6 Continue to cover the hand in a figure-eight pattern.

Step 7 Keep a sufficient amount of wrap to finish off wrapping around the wrist several times, securing with the Velcro strip.

Always wear hand wraps under your gloves to protect your hands, knuckles and wrists. Hand wraps alone generally give enough protection when hitting the speed bag and double-end bag.

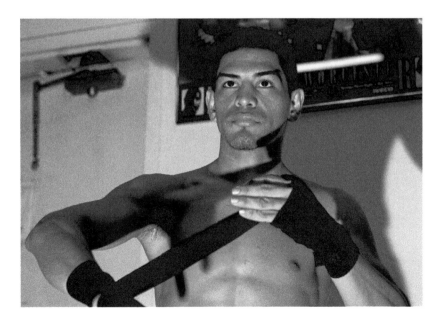

Protect your hands before every training session.

29

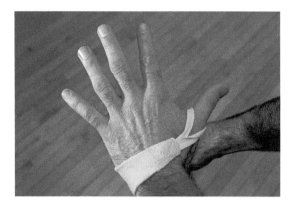

Hand wrapping: step 1.

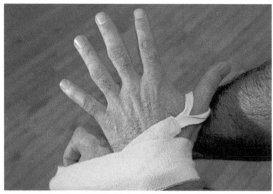

Step 2: wrap twice around the wrist.

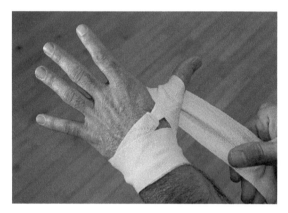

Step 2: wrap once around the thumb.

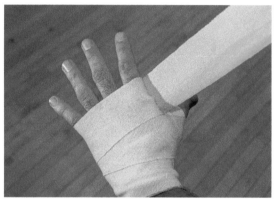

Step 3: wrap around the wrist three to four times.

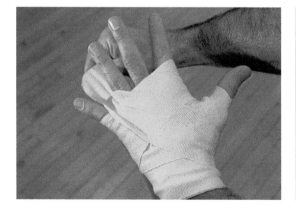

Step 4: wrap between the small finger and the ring finger.

Step 4: wrap between the ring finger and the long finger.

Step 4: wrap between the long finger and the last finger.

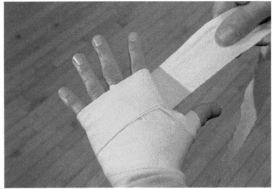

Step 5: wrap around the knuckles several more times.

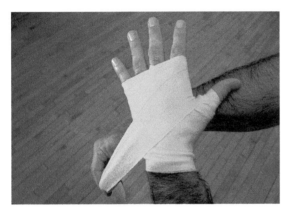

Step 6: start wrapping in a figure of eight a few times.

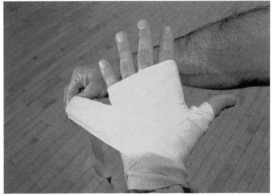

Step 6: continue wrapping in a figure of eight.

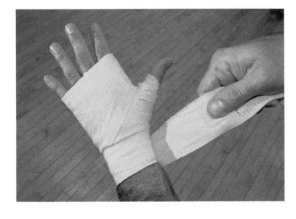

Step 7: finish by securing the wrap around the wrist.

Ensure a snug fit.

Wrapping Your Hands for a Professional Match

Professional boxers always wrap their hands differently when preparing for a fight and some boxers prefer to wrap their hands for training sessions as they would for a boxing match. Depending on the demands of training that day, the coach and boxer may decide to use the more protective wrapping method.

In an actual fight, professional boxers wear 8oz or 10oz gloves, which have less padding. Hitting an opponent who is not wearing headgear with 8oz or 10oz gloves can cause a tremendous force upon the small bones in the hands and wrists. Specific guidelines and certain restrictions are followed and your coach will assist in the way the hands are to be wrapped. Plenty of gauze and tape are used to wrap the hands in a design to provide maximum support for the wrists and hands.

Types of Glove

Bag gloves

There are a variety of types, designs and weights of boxing gloves available today. Bag gloves and sparring gloves have some major differences. Bag gloves are designed specifically to protect the hand when pounding on the heavy bag or throwing punches at focus mitts. They should not be worn in sparring sessions. Bag gloves are thicker and denser at the knuckle area and are typically made with a less expensive synthetic material. They are made to hold up to the wear and tear of hitting the heavy bag. Bag gloves range from 8oz to 16oz and have Velcro wrist fasteners.

Wrapped and ready to spar.

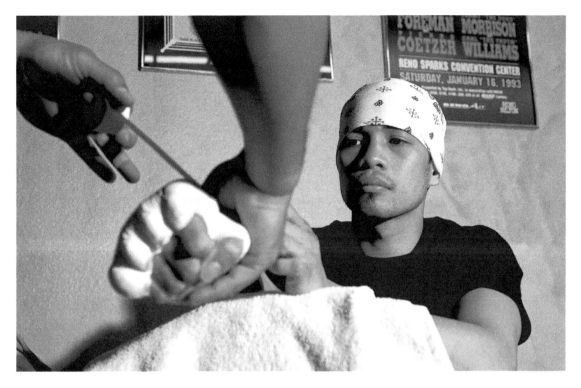

Donaire gets his hands wrapped.

Mayweather prefers to use heavier gloves when working on the bag.

Sparring gloves

Sparring gloves have extra shock-absorbing foam and are designed to protect the hand when punching and blocking, and also protect your opponent when you make contact. The gloves fit snugly at the wrist to provide joint support. There is also extra padding on the wrist area since the boxer blocks against an oncoming punch with this part of the glove. Sparring gloves are at least 16–20oz and have either a Velcro wrist fastener or are a lace-up style.

Use the specific style of glove only for what it is designed. Sparring gloves are used in the ring and should not be used when hitting the heavy bag. Use your bag gloves when working out on the various bags and training on focus mitts. Never use bag gloves when sparring, only use sparring gloves.

Competition boxing gloves

Competition gloves used in amateur boxing are often red or blue, with the knuckle portion of the glove marked in white to assist fight judges in recognizing scoring blows.

Amateur boxing gloves have to be approved by one of the National Boxing Associations and are 12oz, 14oz or 16oz in size and are determined by your weight class. Professional gloves are generally 8–10oz in weight, with lace-up fasteners, and are taped for extra wrist support.

The Heavy Bag

Types of Heavy Bag

There is a large selection of heavy bags available specific to your training needs and individual requirements. They come in a variety of sizes, weights and materials. Leather bags are the most durable but there are numerous types of synthetic, vinyl-coated heavy bags that can take a pounding as well. Canvas bags are the least durable. Heavy bags range from 20 to 70kg (50–150lb) and the heavier they are, the more resistance they afford, and the less forgiving and more jarring they are when hit. A light bag will swing more and be more forgiving.

Hitting the Heavy Bag

There is no opponent when working the heavy bag, so creative imagery can be an effective way to enhance the quality of a specific training session. When training on the heavy bag, imagine you're stepping in the ring with a great champion. Visualize Sergio Martinez rushing out of his corner to defend his title, and give him the fight of his life. Imagine Manny Pacquiao taunting you as he fires jabs and moves away. Put passion and enthusiasm into your workout, making every punch count. Be creative and imaginative, working combinations, slipping and circling the bag.

If you are new to training on the heavy bag, the basics to get you started are listed below (see page 36).

Step 1   Start in the classic on-guard stance in front of the bag. Return to this stance after each punch or punch combination.

Step 2   Establish the distance from which to execute a punch. Throw a few jabs to ensure your arm is extending and the glove is making contact with the centre of the bag.

Step 3   Circle the bag. Continue jabbing and start to build two- and three-punch combinations. Punch and get out!

Step 4   Use the slight swinging motion of the bag to add a sense of realism. If the bag is swinging toward you, step back and maintain the same punch distance. If the bag is swinging away from you, step forward and extend your punches.

Step 5   Practise the moves and combinations until they are technically sound, gradually adding more power to your punches.

Be creative with your combinations.

Establish your punching range with the left jab.

Straight right: fully extend your punches.

Left hook: pivot with your lead foot as you launch your hook

Right uppercut on the bag.

Left uppercut: do not wind up before throwing your uppercuts.

Key Elements to Working the Heavy Bag

Find your range

Focus on the bag, keeping it in view at all times. Establish your punch distance by fully extending your jab arm to the bag and then move back a half step. This is a good starting position. When throwing straight punches hit the bag dead centre. This will prevent it from spinning wildly. Remember it is your legs that move you in and out of range to land your punches. Stay on the balls of your feet ready to move in any direction. Never stand flat-footed. Always be aware of this distance from the bag and visualize it as your opponent. Keep the bag at arm's reach at all times, moving with the bag. Do not wait for the bag to come to you. Follow the bag forward if it is swinging away from you and step back if it is coming toward you. Straight punches set up your short, power punches, so you must use your legs to move in closer to the bag to throw hooks and uppercuts. Remember: move into range, punch the bag and move out again.

Working the bag in a southpaw stance.

Snap your punches.

Snap your punches

Snap your punches; do not push them. Pushing your punches will make the bag swing excessively. Do not allow your fist to make contact with the bag for too long. This is a lazy punch. A sharp punch will jolt the bag, but will not move it as much. As soon as your punch makes contact with the bag, quickly return to the on-guard position, ready to launch your next punch. Your arm should be near full extension when your punch makes contact with the bag. Keeping your arms relaxed in the on-guard position will assist in throwing fast snapping punches. Breathe naturally and exhale as you launch your punch.

Stay busy

Experienced boxers are always throwing punches when working the heavy bag, resting for only a few seconds in between throws. One of the worst habits that can be developed on the heavy bag is taking long breaks between punches. Beginners often throw a few punches and then stand or walk around to catch their breath. If you need a short rest,

Stay busy.

continue moving your feet and throw light punches. Real fights do not have long periods of inactivity. Work the entire three-minute round, punching and moving. Stay busy and keep moving, and emulate a real fight situation.

Mix it up

Vary the speed, tempo and selection. Visualize your opponent's punches coming at you. Visualize opportunities to throw counterpunches. Your punches need to have a logical order to them. You need to have a plan and employ a variety of punches and punch combinations in order to improve.

Basic Heavy Bag Combinations

Double Jabs   Execute a double jab by 'flicking' the first jab as rapidly as possible and following with a second jab. The first jab sneaks in and sets the target up for an even faster follow-up jab. The second jab is launched immediately after the first jab approximately one-third the distance from the target. The arm does not retract all the way to on-guard position. Double jabs have a surprise element to them, as the opponent does not expect the second jab. They are also effective in setting up power shots, such as the straight right.

The One-Two   A classic combination: a crisp left jab, followed by a straight right in quick succession. Move around the back and repeat the combination.

Jab to the Body–Jab to the Head   Use your legs to lower your body position and fire a quick jab to the body (just below mid-point on the heavy bag). Adjust your body position and immediately fire a jab to the head region. When changing positions for a body shot or a head shot, the movement needs to be fluid and in control. A natural follow-up punch could be a straight right.

One-Two–Hook   Start by throwing a fast one-two combination moving you closer to the bag. Finish the combination by throwing a left hook. Move away and get ready for your next series of punches. Your straight punches put you in the proper range to land your short punches.

Intermediate/Advanced Combinations

One-Two–Double Left Hook   Lower your body position to throw a one-two to the body. This will put you in the perfect position to land a left hook to the body and another left hook to the head. Your two hooks have to be rapid-fire and the legs must push the body up to land the second hook to the head.

Left Jab–Right to the Body–Left Hook to the Jaw   This combination challenges your quickness, because it requires you to throw to the head, then to the body, and back to the head. Throw a left jab to the head, bend the legs lowering your body and launch a powerful right to the body, raise the body up again and throw a strong left hook to the jaw. Bring your hands back to the on-guard position after every punch is thrown.

Left Jab–Left Hook–Straight Right–Left Hook   Move in with a quick left jab to the head. Immediately throw a quick left hook to the head. Follow with a straight right to the head. Finish with another left hook to the head. Step back and move.

Straight Right–Left Hook–Straight Right–Left Uppercut   Most combinations start by throwing the left jab first, but this four-punch combination starts by throwing your right-hand power punch first. Launch a lead right hand to the head, followed by a left hook. Throw another straight right and finish with a left uppercut to the chin.

Feint Left–Straight Right–Left Hook–Right Uppercut   Feint with the left jab, and then quickly throw a straight right to the head. Follow with a left hook and right uppercut to the chin. Practise working feints into other punch combinations.

One-Two–One-Two–Left Hook–Straight Right –Double Jab   Lower your body as you throw a quick four-punch flurry to the body (one-two, one-two), then throw a left hook to the head and a strong straight right to the head. As you move away throw a double jab to the head. Bring the hands back in the on-guard position for the next series of punches.

Flurries   A fast series of flurries can surprise your opponent. Practise throwing multiple rapid-fire flurries every round, focusing on speed, not power.

Shoe-shining   This is another old-school term that refers to a series of quick punches. Start by punching near the bottom of the heavy bag and gradually work your way up to the top of the heavy bag and then back down again. Ten punches to the top and ten punches to the bottom. Use the legs to raise and lower the body.

Putting it all Together

We cannot overemphasize the importance of working the bag as if you are in the ring and facing your opponent. Focus on your timing and find your own rhythm. Maintain balance when punching and moving around the bag. Gradually increase the power and intent to your punches, developing smooth transitions from one move to the next. Mix up your punches and combinations and do not be predictable.

Heavy Bag Drills

Speed sprints

The purpose of speed sprints is to improve punch speed, upper body power and endurance, and challenge the cardio-respiratory system. These timed punch interval workouts imitate the stresses placed on the shoulders, back, arms and core muscles during a boxing match.

Keep the feet stationary as you face the bag square on. The body weight is kept on the balls of your feet, abdominal muscles are held tight and the knees stay relaxed. Both shoulders should be an equal distance from the bag. Hit the bag in a left-right, left-right rhythm, extending your punches. Keep the punches quick and fast, without any pauses between them. Aim for a high volume of punches executed with speed and precision.

Sprint for fifteen seconds and recover for fifteen seconds. Work up to twenty-five-second sprints, resting for the same amount of time as you sprint. In between sprints breathe deeply and allow the body to recover for the next series of sprints.

Speed sprints are a quick succession of punches thrown in rapid short bursts.

Sprints: deliver straight punches.

Throw your punches as fast as possible.

Focus on throwing crisp punches to the centre of the bag.

Sample speed sprint

Sprint 1	15s	Recover	15s
Sprint 2	15s	Recover	15s
Sprint 3	15s	Recover	15s

Three-minute sprint and move drill

This drill alternates between smoothly moving around the bag and throwing a quick succession of punches. Begin with a five-second punching sprint, followed by moving around the bag for ten seconds with your hands in the on-guard position. Alternate this pattern of punching for five seconds and moving for ten seconds for a full three-minute round.

Power/speed sprint

This challenging drill is performed for the last minute of a three-minute round. For the first two minutes work the bag with plenty of movement and throw fast punch combinations. For the last minute address the bag straight on and sprint at speed for five seconds as fast as possible, and then without stopping switch to power sprints (hit as hard as you can), for five seconds. Alternate speed sprints with power sprints until the end of the round.

Go all out when performing sprints.

Heavy bag ladder drill

Start by throwing twelve sharp jabs at the heavy bag, keeping the throws as fast as possible. Now move around the bag, keeping your hands up for about six seconds. Move in and throw eleven crisp jabs, move back and around again for another six seconds and then repeat with ten jabs. When moving between your punch sequences move side-to-side, changing direction and staying active. Continue decreasing the number of jabs until you are throwing just one jab. This is the first ladder. For the next ladder, start with throwing twelve straight rights. Put some power behind these punches. Next throw eleven straight rights, move, ten straight rights, nine straight rights

---

COMMON ERRORS AND QUICK FIXES

Error: Stance is too close to the heavy bag and straight punches are not fully extended.

Quick fix: Stand slightly more than a jab's length away from the bag. Move forward as you execute. When you throw straight left and straight right punches your arm should almost be fully extended upon impact.

Error: 'Pushing' punches instead of 'snapping' them. Not only will this make the bag swing wildly, it is a bad habit you do not want to develop.

Quick fix: Quickly snap your punches off the bag as soon as the glove makes contact. Fire your punches straight out from the on-guard position and straight back. Focus on throwing crisp punches to the centre of the bag.

Error: Not moving after executing a series of punches.

Quick fix: You must constantly be moving when boxing. Circle the bag in between your punch combinations, working on footwork.

Error: Dropping your hands after punching decreases the efficiency of the punches and leaves the head exposed. As a boxer becomes fatigued, it is harder to keep the hands up high.

Quick fix: Always keep the fists in the on-guard position. Condition your arms so they do not become fatigued. Use a mirror to recognize when you are dropping your fists.

and so on. The final ladder works on the one-two punch combination. Start by throwing twelve one-twos, move, eleven one-twos, move, all the way to one one-two combination.

Working on straight punches challenges your straight punch technique, movement, endurance and physical conditioning. Aim to complete this drill in less than six minutes.

The Speed Bag

The speed bag is a vital tool for building hand–eye coordination, punching speed and accuracy. A swivel hook below a horizontal platform suspends this small bag and allows for free rotational movement. Speed bags come in various sizes ranging from 35cm (14in) to around 20cm (8in). The smaller bags move faster and rebound quickly, making them the most difficult to hit.

Hitting the Speed Bag

Hitting the speed bag is all about developing a smooth rhythm. The basic or 'triplet' rhythm is the most common. When you strike the bag, it will rebound three times, forward–back–forward. 'Strike' the bag and it will move away from you and hit the other side of the platform (strike 1). The bag will then rebound towards you and hit the platform closest to you (strike 2). The bag rebounds again and hits the other side of the platform (strike 3). As the bag starts to come toward you again, it is in the proper position to be hit and the sequence (strike 1–2–3) is repeated.

The triplet rhythm also refers to the three sounds the speed bag makes on the platform. There is a distinctive sound as the speed bag hits the platform and as you become more proficient the 1–2–3 rhythms become faster. On hitting the bag, the first, and loudest, sound is the bag hitting the back of the

Pacman works on his timing on the speed bag.

Stand square to the bag.

Strike with the knuckle portion of your fist. The bag hits the back of the platform.

The bag rebounds toward you and hits the front of the platform.

The bag rebounds again and hits the back of the platform.

platform. The bag rebounds to the front of the platform for the second sound and the third rebound on the back of the platform is the softness sound. Remember: the rhythm is strike 1–2–3, and for every punch the bag will go forward–back–forward, and be ready to hit again.

To begin, stand square in front of the bag and not in the classic boxing stance. The reason you are not in your boxing stance is that you want both arms to have equal reach to the speed bag. Stand slightly closer than arm's length away from the bag. Make sure the bottom of the bag is around eye level, give or take a few centimetres. Most speed bag platforms are adjustable in height, so can be altered as necessary. Ensure the speed bag is not over-inflated, as it will be harder to control and rebound faster. Letting

An open hand will give more control of the speed bag.

Find your rhythm.

out some of the air will slow down the bag slightly and give you more control.

Sometimes it seems as though the speed bag has a mind of its own as it swings off-centre and does not respond to your strikes. How hard you hit the speed bag will influence your ability to keep it under control, so start by using medium-force strikes and add more speed when you are comfortable with the timing. Smaller speed bags are faster and more difficult to hit. They provide a greater challenge for hand–eye coordination and the development of agility. In order to protect your hands and knuckles wear hand wraps when hitting the speed bag.

Open Hand Method

Beginners often hit the speed bag too hard and too fast, and will quickly lose control. Instead of hitting the bag with the knuckles and a closed fist, keep your hands open and hit with the fingers (palm side). The fingers are held wide to give more contact time with the bag and better control, moving the bag in a straight swinging motion. Allow the bag to roll off your fingers. This will help beginners slow down the pace and become familiar with the 'strike 1–2–3' rhythm. Follow steps 1–5 below with open hands.

Proper Form

Step 1 Face the bag straight on. Keep both fists close to the bag. When one hand is striking, the other hand is held ready to follow up.

Step 2 Your fists should travel in small circles as you hit, and follow through in a smooth motion with your punches. Hit the speed bag flush with the knuckles of the fist near the centre of the bag. This will give you greatest control of the swinging motion. If contact is made too soon the bag will jam and stop moving. Making contact too late will create an awkward rhythm and cause the bag to swing wildly.

Step 3 Strike lightly at first to establish a rhythm. A light rhythm will give you greatest control and keep the speed bag on a straight path.

Step 4 Start with a double strike, hitting twice with each hand, left–left–right–right. Striking twice with each fist will give you sufficient time to bring your opposite hand into the correct position.

Step 5 Now move onto single strikes. As you hit the bag with your left fist, the right fist immediately comes up ready to strike. This will be more challenging, as you will be hitting at a faster pace because it is only one strike per fist. Keep the punching motion short and fast using small circles. Do not allow the hands to drop after the strike, but quickly bring them back up close to the bag.

45

Smaller speed bags are more challenging.

COMMON ERRORS AND QUICK FIXES

Error: Hitting the bag with too much force, causing it to spin unpredictably.

Quick fix: Strike the bag lightly, keeping the punch motion short and smooth. Gradually increase the speed as your rhythm and timing become more comfortable.

Error: Not bringing your hands back up after striking the bag, resulting in a chopping motion.

Quick fix: Keeping your hands low will throw your timing off and make it difficult to generate speed. After the strike, follow through in a smooth circular motion up to the start position. When one hand is striking the bag, the other hand is held ready to follow up.

Error: Standing sideways, leading with your left or right foot.

Quick fix: Standing sideways or in a boxing stance will not give you equal reach with both arms. Face the bag square on to work the speed bag.

Stay focused.

Freestyle Rhythm

The method of striking the bag in a freestyle rhythm will happen when you are comfortable going from multiple strikes with each hand to single strikes, effortlessly mixing up the speed and rhythm. Challenge yourself by moving your feet and circling the speed bag while you punch. Change direction, moving to the right and then the left as you throw your punches. Include short bursts of rapid-fire punching, speed sprints and punch as fast as possible, going as fast as possible for twenty to thirty seconds, then go back to a regular rhythm. Repeat more sprints. Several rounds on the speed bag will challenge your upper body endurance, teach you to keep your hands up, and improve your hand–eye coordination.

The Double-End Striking Bag

These small, lightweight, inflatable round bags are suspended from the ceiling to the floor, anchored by bungee cords. They come in a variety of sizes and, like the speed bag, the smaller double-end bags will be more difficult to hit as you attempt to land punches accurately. Double-end bags will react most effectively when filled with a moderate amount of air pressure.

Hitting the double-end bag helps develop coordination, speed and accuracy of your punches.

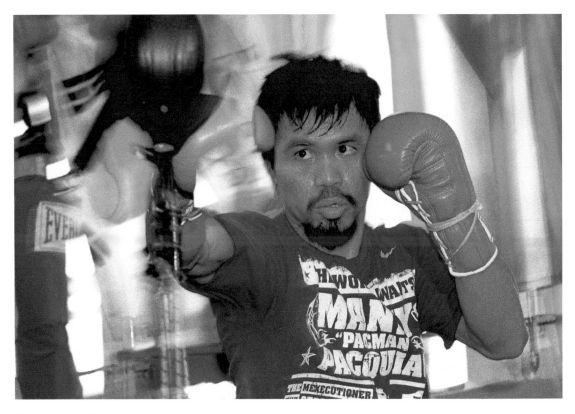

Hands on-guard. Be ready to react.

Double-end bags are specifically designed to improve the timing, speed and accuracy of your punches. Save your punch power for the heavy bag. Standing in the boxing stance, the double-end bag should be approximately eye level. This is the correct height to start your double-end bag workout. Wear your bag gloves when hitting the bag. Gloves will have a larger contact area and more padding, giving you more control. When wearing just hand wraps, the bag will react faster with less control. Keep your hands high in the on-guard position and ready to react, as the bag may rebound and hit you.

When you strike the bag it will move quickly away. As the bag rebounds toward you, evade it by slipping it or striking it again. The timing and rhythm are totally different from hitting any other bag.

Punch Drill

Address the bag straight on. Throw quick straight punches (one-twos), hitting the bag in the centre. Hit the bag lightly at first, at a moderate pace. Aim to tap continuously for thirty to sixty seconds, without allowing the bag to rebound fully. As you reduce the time between strikes, you can add more speed to your punches, and try double punches (double left, double right).

Basic Slip Drill

Left jab (left jab—slip right)

Step 1   Stand in front of the bag in your boxing stance, weight centred on the balls of your feet and your hands up, ready to strike.

Throw sharp punches to the centre of the bag.

Keep your hands up.

Step 2   Throw a sharp left jab and, as the bag rebounds, slip to the right. Immediately return to your upright stance. Aim for the centre of the bag, so it will move away in a straight line and directly back at you. Continue practising this drill until you feel comfortable with your timing. Focus on proper technique, not power.

Basic Double-End Bag Combinations

Double jabs (double jab–slip right)

Start by throwing two jabs. The second jab must be thrown quickly before the bag rebounds fully. Slip to the right after the second jab hits the bag. Keep your hands up and quickly recover to an upright position.

One-two combo (one-two–slip left)

Throw a fast one-two and slip to the left. As you throw the straight right, continue with the rotation of the body, slipping to the left and allowing the bag to go over your right shoulder.

One-two, one-two, slip, slip (one-two, one-two, slip left, slip right)

Throw a left jab, a straight right; another left jab and straight right, followed by a slip to the left and a

Execute your slips quickly.

slip to the right. Return to the on-guard position to throw the combination again. Remember that the rebound action of the bag is simulating an incoming punch, so keep your hands up and execute your slips quickly.

Throw punches from multiple angles.

COMMON ERRORS AND QUICK FIXES

Error: Hitting the double-end too hard, causing it to move erratically.

Quick fix: Unlike the heavy bag, where it is easy to hit the target, you must be accurate when throwing at the double-end bag. Strike the bag in a controlled manner with light, crisp punches. Save your power punches for either the uppercut bag or heavy bag.

Error: Exaggerating the slipping motion, causing you to be out of position and off-balance.

Quick fix: With your hands in the on-guard position, move your body just enough to avoid the rebounding bag. Always keep eye contact with the bag. Slips should be subtle, in control, and always on-balance.

Freestyle

Practise your slips, and mix up the punches. Use your footwork to manoeuvre around the double-end bag, creating another dimension to your training. This will simulate 'sparring' against an opponent. Focus on rapid-succession punching. Your timing, accuracy and your ability to gauge distance will be tested.

The Uppercut Bag

Uppercut bags are similar in design to a heavy bag but are hung horizontally, allowing you to execute the punch properly and land uppercuts with the knuckle portion of the glove landing flush on the bag. Uppercuts are the least utilized punch in boxing and using this bag is a great way to develop the punch.

Work on speed. Save your power for the heavy bag.

Standing in front of the bag in the boxing stance, elbows tucked, practise throwing short uppercuts with both hands. Make sure you land with the knuckle portion of your glove and remember not to wind up or pull back before you launch your uppercut.

The left and right sides of the uppercut bag are good for practising hooks. Standing slightly off to the right side of the bag in your boxing stance, throw a left uppercut followed by a right hook. This allows you to practise a smooth transition of your weight from the front foot (as you throw your left upper-cut) to the back foot (as you throw your right hook). Now, stand on the left side of the bag in your boxing stance and work on throwing a short right uppercut

Land your punches flush against the bag.

Move into range before launching your uppercut.

followed by a left hook, with the transfer of weight from the back foot to the front foot.

In a boxing match, uppercuts can be the most difficult punches to land. Set up your uppercuts by throwing straight punches first (left jabs or straight rights).

Basic Uppercut Combinations

Combination one: jab–jab–uppercut
Standing in the on-guard stance in front of the bag, throw two quick jabs as you move in closer, then throw a short right uppercut. Repeat.

Combination two: one-two–uppercut
Throw a one-two (left jab and straight right). Once your straight right has made contact with the bag you are in the correct position to throw the left uppercut. After landing your left uppercut, quickly move away and repeat. You can build on this combination by adding a right uppercut (one-two–left uppercut–right uppercut).

The Hook/Uppercut Wall-Mounted Bag

The unique shape of wall-mounted bags allows you to practise punches from multiple angles, particularly

---

COMMON ERRORS AND QUICK FIXES

Error: Landing with the palm side of the glove on the bag, instead of with the knuckles. This compromises the wrist and is an ineffective uppercut.

Quick fix: Hit with the knuckle part of the fist. Bend the knees and lower the body to get under the bag before you throw the punch. By keeping the elbows in and driving the punch straight up, you will strike with your knuckles.

Error: Sloppy execution, such as winding up or looping your uppercut.

Quick fix: Delivery of this punch is fast and tight. No wasted energy. Keep the neck and shoulders relaxed and the elbows tucked in as you throw the uppercut. Make quick contact with the bag and return to the boxing stance swiftly.

---

hooks and uppercuts. Unlike the heavy bag, where you can circle the bag and throw your combinations, the wall-mounted bag is the best place to practise your range, moving into and out of position and throwing a variety of punch combinations. These bags have circular target zones to aim your punches at, including a body zone and a head zone.

Body punches.

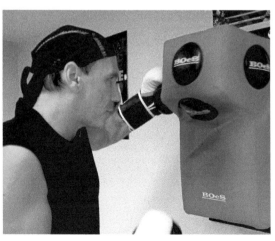

Practising hooks on the wall-mounted bag.

Develop your hook and uppercut combinations.

Basic Combinations

Combination one: one-two–left hook–right uppercut

Throw a one-two (left jab–straight right) to the body. Follow with a left hook to the head and finish with a right uppercut. Remember to use your legs, bending the knees to throw the body punches.

Combination two: left jab–right uppercut–left hook

Start with a left jab to the head, immediately follow up with a right uppercut and then end with a left hook to the head. Move back after landing the hook and set up for the next combination. Always keep moving.

Mastering all of the various bags will challenge your speed, power, agility, hand–eye coordination and timing. Whatever bag you are training on, focus on executing the moves correctly to increase your skill level and improve your physical conditioning. Practise in the same way that you want to perform.

COMMON ERRORS AND QUICK FIXES

Error: Staying too close to the wall-mounted bag after throwing a punch combination.

Quick fix: Remind yourself to punch and get out. Step back more than a jab's length away before you throw your next combination.

Error: Throwing sloppy punches, hitting the edges of the wall-mounted bag.

Quick fix: Keep your eyes on the bag, landing sharp, crisp punches on the circular target zones.

CHAPTER 4

FOCUS MITT TRAINING

Speed is the enemy of every opponent, but not everyone has the reflexes of Floyd Mayweather Jr or Manny Pacquiao. When you work on focus mitts with an accomplished trainer, precise synchronization of speed, accuracy and power can be developed. This dynamic training environment is the closest thing to replicating an actual sparring session or bout. The training can be designed to meet the specific needs of a fighter, improving all aspects of boxing ability. Focus mitt training sharpens both the offensive and defensive skills, and it is an essential training method for successful boxers.

Canadian boxing coach, Russ Anber, says:

> To me there are two levels of training a fighter. There are things you have to do to condition a fighter. There are things you have to do to teach a fighter. I do whatever I have to do to teach and then condition.

Focus mitt training gets the job done on both fronts.

Focus mitts replicate real fight situations.

Dynamic training improves timing and accuracy.

Working with a Partner

If you are not working with a trainer, choose a partner with a similar ability level, and work together to develop the focus mitt skills.

Learn Both Roles

You will benefit from working on focus mitts whether you are the puncher/boxer or the catcher/trainer, and there is an art to communicating and working together as a team. The catcher must give clear and concise directions to the puncher and the puncher must respond quickly and skilfully. As a catcher you are able to observe if the puncher is throwing sloppy punches or crisp punches, moving with awkward foot placement or using balanced fluid footwork. You can detect what moves are effective and successful, and give feedback to the puncher. The puncher is able to learn from the feedback, perfecting their movement and punching style.

The Catcher

The role of the catcher is an important one. The catcher controls the action and sets the pace by calling out punch combinations. When holding the focus mitts, the arm position is similar to the on-guard boxing stance, except the palms are turned toward your partner ready to receive a punch. The elbows are slightly bent to absorb the impact of the incoming punches. To maintain stability the body, leg and foot positions are held in the classic boxing stance. The catcher must always keep their eyes on the puncher, clearly communicate the combination to be executed, and give feedback to the puncher.

The Puncher

As the puncher, you now have a moving target in front of you. Stand in your boxing stance ready to respond quickly to your catcher's punch combination commands. Start by standing slightly more than

Catcher and puncher work together as a team.

a jab length away from the catcher, looking at the focus mitts and listening for the instructions. Focus on throwing all punches with proper technique, accuracy and speed. Be alert and be ready to move in and out as you throw your punches, all the while staying light on your feet. Concentrate on the technical execution of your punches. Add speed and complexity later.

Working Together

The catcher must position the mitts ready to receive each punch. For the straight punches the catcher holds the mitt palm side toward the puncher. Catch the left jab with the left focus mitt and the straight right with the right focus mitt. The catcher holds the left focus mitt with the palm facing inward to catch the left hook and holds the right focus mitt palm down to catch the right uppercut. It is important not to just hold the focus mitts to catch the punch, but to actively 'feed' the mitts into the punches. This provides the proper feel, distance and resistance for the puncher. For the catcher, actively feeding the punch will offset some of the force of the incoming blow and provides stability. It also reduces the occurrence of injuries to both the puncher and catcher.

Start by practising the basic punches. The following combinations are based on the puncher starting in the classic boxing stance with the left foot forward. Left-hand punches (jabs) are thrown to the catcher's left focus mitt and the right-hand punches (straight rights) are thrown to the catcher's left focus mitt. Left hooks are thrown to the left focus mitt. Right uppercuts are thrown to the right focus mitt. Punching to the opposite mitt creates a more realistic rotation of the body and develops strength in the core.

It is critical that the puncher waits for the punching combination commands from the catcher before throwing at the focus mitts. The catcher decides on the combinations and sets the pace of the rounds. As the puncher becomes comfortable with punch accuracy and response time, more combinations can be added, including forward, backward, and side-to-side movements.

Basic Drills

Building Combinations

Communication between the catcher and the puncher is of utmost importance. Each must keep the other in their eyesight. Punchers need to follow the catcher's commands and should not execute any moves that have not been called out by the catcher. The catcher can call basic combinations by using the following number sequence.

1   left jab
2   straight right
3   left hook
4   right uppercut.

Catcher calls 1: puncher executes a left jab.
Catcher calls 2: puncher executes a straight right.
Catcher calls 1, 2: puncher executes a left jab–straight right combination.
Catcher calls 1, 2, 3: puncher executes a left jab–straight right–left hook combination.
Catcher calls 1, 2, 3, 4: puncher executes a left jab–straight right–left hook–right uppercut combination.

It is always good to review the basics, but if you have experience working the mitts with a partner of equal experience, go directly to working the advanced combinations. If you are just beginning to work with focus mitts, both the catcher and the puncher need to practise throwing and catching the basic punches to develop technique, reaction time, fluidity and hand–eye coordination. Punchers work on the basics by coming in, throwing the punch called for, and then stepping away and getting ready to throw the next punch.

'Punch and Get Out' Drill

Boxers are constantly looking for opportunities to set up an attack and then quickly move away to guard against counterpunches. This drill focuses on moving into range to deliver punches, and immediately moving out of range ready to set up for the next series of punches. Below, a three-minute round is broken down into divisions, starting with single punches and building up to combinations.

Three-minute round breakdown
Jab (thirty seconds)   For the first thirty seconds the puncher is just working on the jab. The puncher

Left jab delivered to left focus mitt.

Straight right to catcher's right mitt.

Focus mitt turns in to receive left hook.

Mitt angles to receive right uppercut.

Left uppercut to left focus mitt.

emphasis is on finding your punch range, becoming comfortable with moving around, and finding your balance. Catchers must be ready to catch and feed the punch. Vary the time you spend moving around before throwing the next punch.

Straight Right (thirty seconds)　For the next thirty seconds, the puncher throws only straight rights at the catcher's focus mitt, again concentrating on moving in and throwing the straight right. The puncher then moves quickly out, taking time to set up for the next punch. Remember to drive off the trailing foot as you launch the straight right and return to the balanced boxing stance as quickly as possible. Repetition of this punch will reinforce your straight right punch range and develop muscle memory of the movement. Continue to vary the time you spend moving in and out before throwing the next punch. Catchers must be ready to catch and feed the punch.

One-Two Combination (thirty seconds) The puncher now combines the jab and straight right for a one-two combination. Move in toward the catcher, throw the one-two combination and then move away, returning to the on-guard stance and obtaining balance. Work on bringing the left

starts with the hands held high in the on-guard position. He throws left jabs at the catcher's focus mitt, concentrating on moving in, throwing the jab and then moving out, taking time to set up for the next punch. Snap the jab straight toward the focus mitt and return quickly to the on-guard position. The

jab back to protect the head before launching the straight right. Focus on smooth transitions from one punch to the next. The catcher has both mitts in a ready position to receive the quick one-two.

One-Two-Three Combination (thirty seconds)   The puncher throws a one-two-three combination (left jab–straight right–left hook). The puncher steps in to land the left jab, follows immediately with a straight right and finishes with a short left hook. After the left hook is landed, step away, immediately moving around. Repeat the sequence. The catcher must have the mitts ready at the proper angle to receive these punches. The puncher must focus on executing strong crisp punches, moving in and out to reinforce range and movement. Find a rhythm with one punch flowing into the next punch.

One-Two-Three-Four Combination (thirty seconds)   Puncher throws a one-two-three-four combination (left jab–straight right–left hook–right uppercut). This four-punch combination allows you to work on the smooth transitions of the four punches. Start punching lightly, concentrating on the technical execution of each punch. Add speed later. Puncher steps in with the left jab, then a straight right, follows with a short left hook and finishes up with the right uppercut. Remember, after you have landed your final punch step away and keep moving around. Repeat the sequence. The catcher must have the focus mitts ready a split second before receiving the punch.

Four-Punch Flurry (thirty seconds)   For the last thirty seconds of the round, throw a quick four-punch flurry, one-two, one-two (left–right, left–right) and then move out quickly. The focus is on quickness, not power. Finish the round strong, keeping the punches crisp and not dropping your hands. Punch and get out!

Listed below are some common errors and suggestions on how to improve your game.

Ensure that hand–eye coordination is developed before moving on to the more advanced focus mitt drills.

COMMON ERRORS AND QUICK FIXES

Error: Boxer stands still after throwing a punch combination.

Quick fix: Always move out of range after punching, ready for the next combination.

Error: The catcher holds the focus mitts with straight arms.

Quick fix: Catching arms should be slightly bent at the elbow joint, allowing the arms to absorb the punch. 'Feed' the punch by moving the mitt forward slightly to meet the incoming punch.

Error: Throwing punches with too much force, leading to improper technique.

Quick fix: Not every punch has to be a knockout punch. The main purpose of focus mitt training is to improve speed, technique and accuracy. Efficient, powerful punches come from proper technique.

Advanced Focus Mitts

Focus mitt drills allow you to work on timing and accuracy while mimicking real fight situations. Your trainer can see every move that you make and provide instant feedback. Once you feel comfortable with the basic combinations, begin to incorporate more advanced drills. These combinations involve the catcher simulating throwing punches and require intense focus. Respect the catcher, work together and pay attention.

Defensive Moves

Defensive moves are integral to the advanced focus mitt drills, and add a sense of realism to the workout. Blocking, parrying, ducking and slipping a punch are essential defensive techniques that must be mastered.

Blocking
Blocking is a defensive move that prevents punches from landing on the face, head or body area. Your

arms and gloves are used to absorb the impact of the punch. To block a straight punch, hold your fists with the palm side of the gloves turned in toward your face. The arms and hands are held up high and tight, with sufficient space between the gloves to see your opponent. To block punches to the body, the arms are lowered and positioned to displace the force of the oncoming punch. When the punch arrives, stay relaxed and ready for the contact.

Blocking combination

Block–block, one–two   The puncher keeps the gloves tight against the head, standing in an on-guard position. The catcher throws a left and right hook, lightly tapping the puncher's gloves. The palm side of the focus mitts taps the puncher's gloves. The puncher blocks with the left glove, then the right glove, and returns with a quick one-two to the focus mitts.

COMMON ERRORS AND QUICK FIXES

Error: Catcher throws with too much intent.

Quick fix: For blocking drills the catcher's job is to simulate an incoming blow or punch. It should be a sharp tap to the gloves. There should be some realistic intent when simulating punches, but there is no need to hit too hard.

Error: Puncher starts to pull the gloves away from the head when blocking an incoming mitt.

Quick fix: The puncher's gloves must remain tight to the sides of the head, without any space. The head is not protected when the glove is held away from the head. Stay relaxed, eyes on your partner and do not flinch.

Puncher blocks incoming left strike.

Puncher blocks incoming right strike.

Puncher counters with a left jab.

Puncher follows up with a straight right.

Parrying

Parrying involves 'catching' and slightly redirecting an incoming punch. Unlike blocking, where the punch is simply neutralized, parrying redirects the momentum of the incoming punch, putting your opponent off-balance and creating opportunities to counter-punch. In order to parry a punch, 'catch' the punch with the palm side of your glove and then, with a sharp, strong movement, deflect it. To parry a left jab, use the palm side of your right glove to catch the punch. Quickly bring your glove back to the on-guard position. To parry an incoming right, catch the punch with the inside of the left glove and then return to the on-guard position. Timing of the catch is essential. Do not anticipate and over-react by pawing or reaching for an incoming punch.

Parrying combination

Parry–Jab   The boxer stands in the on-guard position ready to parry an incoming jab from the catcher. With some realistic intent, the catcher throws a light jab straight toward the puncher's gloves. The boxer parries the jab and throws a jab to the catcher's right target mitt. Communicate and give the puncher lots of time to see the punch coming, in order to set up the 'catch' with their palm portion of the right glove. As you perfect the timing, increase the speed of the jab and parry.

Ducking

Ducking is a relatively simple defensive move. Quickly bend the knees, lowering the head and dropping

---

COMMON ERRORS AND QUICK FIXES

Error: Pawing, reaching or slapping at an incoming straight punch, leaving your head exposed.

Quick fix: Wait and calculate the correct time to deflect and redirect the incoming punch.

---

the body so the punch goes over the top of your head. Rapidly return to your on-guard position. Keep your back straight and your eyes on your opponent. To duck a straight punch, move straight down and prepare for an offensive attack. To duck a hook, lower your body and shift your weight, moving out of harm's way. Properly executing a duck will allow you to avoid the incoming punch and set you up for a counterpunch.

Ducking combination

One-Two–Duck–Straight Right   The puncher throws a one-two combination at the focus mitts. The catcher then simulates a left hook. The puncher bends the legs and ducks under the left hook and follows up with a straight right.

As you duck under the punch do not look at the floor. Keep your eyes on the catcher. The catcher needs to simulate the hook in a controlled manner, allowing the puncher to duck underneath. Once

Boxer parries the left jab.

Boxer returns with a sharp left jab to the catcher's right mitt.

COMMON ERRORS AND QUICK FIXES

Error: Ducking too low. Ducking too low will waste energy and make it very difficult to throw an effective counterpunch.

Quick fix: Stay balanced and bend your knees just enough to avoid the punch. Practise in front of a mirror.

Error: Bending at the waist too far forward and not lowering with the legs. When bending forward and downward it is difficult to see your opponent's punches and it places you off-balance.

Quick fix: Always maintain eye contact with your opponent and lower the body by bending the knees.

both are comfortable with the timing of the duck, speed it up.

Slipping

Slipping is an essential defensive technique, but also the most difficult to learn. You must react quickly when slipping, as your body is moving to avoid the incoming punch.

To slip a punch, bend slightly at the waist and knees and move the body to the left or the right so the punches miss you. Always keep the hands up in the on-guard position in case your slip was not effective. To slip a left jab, the head, body and shoulders move as one unit to the right. With a slip to the right, the tendency is to lean back on your trailing foot. Keep your body weight forward and stay off your heels. To slip a straight right, dip to the left, moving your head, body and shoulders together. Always return

Puncher throws a jab at the focus mitt.

Puncher follows with a straight right.

Catcher simulates a left hook and puncher ducks under.

Puncher returns with a straight right.

to your balanced boxing position. Unlike blocking or parrying, slipping punches leaves both hands free to counterpunch.

Slipping combination

One-two–slip–slip   The puncher throws a left jab followed by a straight right at the catcher. The catcher responds by throwing a left jab aiming for the puncher's left shoulder. The puncher slips to the right to avoid the punch. The catcher throws a straight right aiming at the puncher's right shoulder and the puncher slips to the left to avoid the punch. The puncher continues to throw a one-two at the catcher, with the catcher responding with a one-two aimed at the puncher's shoulders. The puncher slips to the left, then to the right to avoid the punches.

If you are having difficulty getting into a rhythm when slipping, have the catcher just throw left jabs

with the puncher slipping to his right. The puncher then throws just straight rights with the puncher slipping to his left. Practise this until you feel comfortable with the movement.

COMMON ERRORS AND QUICK FIXES

Error: Over-slipping, causing the body to be off-balance and out of position. This may put you on the back of your heels instead of on the balls of your feet.

Quick fix: Practise in front a mirror. Stay on the balls of the feet and focus on your centre of balance.

Error: Taking your eyes off your partner or looking at the floor.

Quick fix: Always keep your eyes on your partner in order to respond quickly.

Boxer throws a left jab.

Boxer follows with a straight right.

Catcher simulates a left jab and boxer slips to the left.

Catcher simulates a straight right and boxer slips to the right.

Building Advanced Combinations

Combination one
Parry-jab-jab–slip-right cross

Puncher parries incoming jab.

Break up this combination into two parts and practise each one separately before putting them together.

Step 1 Parry-jab-jab. Catcher simulates a jab; puncher parries the jab and throws two quick jabs back to the catcher's right focus mitt. (Catcher throws at three-quarter speed.) Repeat several times until the movement flows.

Step 2 Slip-right cross. Catcher throws a jab; puncher slips to the right side and counters with a right cross. Try this several times before you put it together.

Step 3 Put it all together. Parry the incoming jab and then fire back with two quick jabs. Slip the second incoming jab and finish with a right cross.

Fire two quick jabs. Jab one.

Jab two.

Catcher simulates a jab, puncher slips.

Puncher throws a right cross.

Boxer slips incoming jab.

Combination two
Slip-uppercut–slip-hook

Step 1   Slip-uppercut. Catcher throws a left jab; the puncher slips right (puncher slips a left jab) and then throws a right uppercut. Practise this five or six times.

Step 2   Slip-hook. Catcher throws a straight right and puncher slips to the left and counterpunches with a left hook.

Step 3   Put it all together. Slip-uppercut–slip-hook.

Boxer throws a right uppercut.

Catcher throws a right and the puncher slips to the left.

Boxer throws a left hook.

65

Combination three
One-two–slip–right-left-right

Step 1 Puncher starts this drill with a quick one-two combination.

Step 2 Catcher throws a left jab as puncher slips to the right, avoiding the incoming jab.

Step 3 Puncher counters with three straight punches: right-left-right.

Boxer throws a jab.

Straight right.

Slips incoming jab.

Counters with a straight right.

Left jab.

Straight right.

Combination four
One-two, one-two–slip-slip–left hook-straight right

Step 1   Puncher throws four straight punches: one-two, one-two

Step 2   Puncher slips a left jab and slips a straight right.

Step 3   Puncher finishes with a left hook and a straight right.

Continued overleaf

Start this combo with a fast left jab.

Straight right.

Left jab.

Straight right.

Boxer slips to the right.

Boxer slips to the left.

Counters with a left hook.

Finish with a straight right.

Throw three uppercuts starting with the right.

Combination five (left and below)
Uppercut-uppercut-uppercut–left hook–straight right

Step 1 Catcher holds the mitts in position to receive three uppercuts.
Step 2 Puncher starts with the right uppercut first, then left, then right.
Step 3 Follow with a left hook and finish with a straight right. This five-punch combination should be smooth and controlled.

Left uppercut.

Right uppercut.

Follow with a left hook.

Finish with a straight right.

Start with a crisp left jab.

Follow with a straight right.

Combination six
One-two-three–duck–left hook–straight right

Step 1 Puncher starts by throwing a three-punch combination; left jab, a straight right and a left hook.
Step 2 The catcher simulates a right hook.
Step 3 Puncher ducks under the hook and returns with a left hook and a straight right. Stay balanced when ducking and keep your eyes on your partner.

Left hook.

Duck under right hook.

Keep eyes on partner as you duck under.

Come back with a left hook.

Finish with a straight right.

Start with a jab.

Slip incoming jab to the right.

Combination seven
Jab–slip–right cross–left hook

Step 1   Puncher throws a left jab to the catcher's right mitt.
Step 2   The catcher immediately comes back with a left jab, tapping the puncher on the left shoulder.
Step 3   The puncher quickly slips to the right, pivots back with a right cross and finishes off with a left hook. Be ready to move quickly.

Throw a right cross.

Finish the combination with a left hook.

Combination eight
Block–hook–straight right–block–right–left–right

Step 1 Puncher holds his hands high in the on-guard position, keeping the gloves tight against the head.
Step 2 Catcher simulates a left hook by tapping the puncher's gloves with the inside (cushion side) of the mitt.
Step 3 Puncher blocks the punch then fires back with a quick left hook and straight right.
Step 4 Catcher simulates a straight right by lightly tapping the puncher's gloves.
Step 5 Puncher blocks the punch then fires back with a quick straight right, left jab, and then a straight right.

LEFT: Stay relaxed as you block the incoming hook. RIGHT: Counter with a left hook.

Straight right.

Block the right punch.

Counter with a straight right.

Throw a left jab.

Finish with a straight right.

Body block.

Head block.

Combination nine
**Body block–head block–left hook–
straight right–left hook–slip left–
left hook–straight right**

Step 1   Catcher simulates a left hook to the body
and a left hook to the head with two quick taps of
the focus mitt.

Step 2   Puncher blocks the first shot with the
elbow and immediately raises the fist to block the
head shot.

Throw a left hook.

Throw a straight right.

Throw a second left hook.

Step 3   Puncher throws a left hook, a straight right and another left hook.
Step 4   Catcher throws a straight right and the puncher slips to their left.
Step 5   Puncher returns with a left hook and a straight right.

When practising defensive drills such as blocking, parrying and slipping, stay on-guard and make your moves concise and smooth.

Practise combinations until they become smooth and natural, with the punches flowing easily from one to the next. The moves should be realistic and have a purpose. Try not to get hung up on working just fancy combinations. Break up multiple punch sequences by going back to the basics: jabbing, moving and throwing single punches.

Catcher throws a right and puncher slips to their left.

Puncher comes back with a left hook.

Finish with a straight right.

Body Protector/Trainer's Vest

A body protector vest is a great tool to include with focus mitt drills. It is a thick foam padded vest worn by the coach that adds another dimension to the training. Boxers can now work body punches into the mix. When you launch your straight punches aim for the centre of the vest. Aim the hooks to the side of the vest. Practise combinations that involve throwing body punches (to the body protector) and head punches (to the focus mitts). All body shots make contact with the body vest and all head shots make contact with the focus mitts.

Training vests take focus mitt training to the next level.

Work body punches into your focus mitt combinations.

Basic Body Vest Combination

One-two-three combination to the body
Left jab–straight right–left hook (body)
Throw a quick jab, followed by a straight right aiming at the centre of the body vest. Finish up with a left hook to the side of the body vest.

One-two to the body, one-two to the head
Left jab–straight right (body)–jab–straight right (head)   Snap a jab, followed by a straight right to the body vest, bending at the knees to lower the punches and then immediately throw a jab and a straight right to the focus mitts.

Focus Mitt Sprints

Focus mitt sprints will challenge your aerobic endurance. Work the basic punches over and over, focusing on speed and accuracy.

Catcher

The catcher prepares to receive a series of fast punches. Stand straight on to the puncher. Hold the mitts at the correct angle for each punch: straight on to receive straight left and right punches, palms in to receive hooks, and palms facing down to catch the uppercuts.

Puncher

With your hands in the on-guard position and your body facing straight to the catcher, stay on the balls of your feet with your body weight slightly forward. Be ready to execute the punches as fast as possible, while still maintaining good punching technique. Start by throwing straight lefts and rights, using your full reach. Throw hooks, rotating through the body. Bend your legs and punch up into the focus mitts for uppercuts. Complete this sequence without stopping, throwing straight punches followed directly by hooks and then uppercuts.

Zab Judah practising speed sprints on the focus mitts.

Sample Sprint Interval

Straight punches	20 seconds
Hooks	20 seconds
Uppercuts	20 seconds

If you are training with a partner, switch roles after completing the sprint two times. Do not take a break. Begin with intervals of twenty seconds, increasing to thirty- to forty-second sprints. To add variety, add double straight rights—double straight lefts for twenty seconds, double hooks each side and double uppercuts each side within the sprint times.

Throw straight punches as fast as possible.

Follow with left and right hooks.

Finish with uppercuts.

Freestyle Focus Mitt Training

Trainers use focus mitts to provide dynamic practice and replicate real fight situations. Unlike the heavy bag, you get to train with a target that is constantly moving.

Focus mitt training should always be challenging and not become too routine. It is important to tailor focus mitt workouts to each individual's needs and skill level. With freestyle focus mitt training, combinations are random and the fighter does not always know what to expect. The trainer will improvise combinations and may throw counterpunches with some realistic intent. This allows the fighter to practise different defensive moves and pursue counterpunch opportunities. Focus mitt training should always be physically challenging and mentally engaging.

Focus mitt training should always be challenging.

Mitt training sharpens offensive and defensive skills.

Your trainer can mimic real fight situations.

CHAPTER 5

JUMP ROPE

Float like a Butterfly …

The great Muhammad Ali would dance around the ring, rapidly alternating his feet front and back in a shuffle as he delivered lightning fast combinations. Jump rope was one of the key elements to Ali's leg conditioning and fast footwork training. Jumping rope will help you 'float like a butterfly and sting like a bee.'

Jumping rope develops speed, quickness and agility, placing demands on every muscle in your body, including your core. Foot speed, hand speed and balance are all necessary attributes for a successful boxer, and jumping rope will train your body and develop these skills. It takes time and commitment to master the basic jumps, but once this is accomplished, a wide variety of combinations can be performed. It is a great total-body workout to improve overall conditioning. Jumping rope challenges the cardiovascular system and improves eye–hand–foot coordination, which in turn helps to develop boxing agility and fluidity, lateral movement, explosiveness, hand and foot speed, and timing.

Ricky Hatton developing quickness and agility.

Jumping rope challenges your cardiovascular conditioning.

Choosing the Right Rope

Choosing the proper jump rope is the first consideration. There are different types of ropes to choose from: leather, beaded, weighted or plastic. In order to be successful, the rope has to have a true arc as it rotates through the air. A rope that is very light needs to be rotated faster to obtain this arc movement. A slightly heavier rope, like leather or beaded ropes, allows you to feel the arc of the rope more easily as it rotates. However, be wary of ropes that are too heavy, as they are slow and cumbersome and will require extra effort from the shoulder muscles and wrist area to produce a good rotation. Heavier ropes also have the potential to increase the risk of injuries at the wrists and shoulders. Choose a rope with enough weight that it is easy to turn and less likely to become snagged in your feet. Ensure the handles are comfortable, easy to hold, durable and

The rope should come up to chest level.

allow for smooth movement where the rope and handle meet.

To determine proper rope length, stand with one foot on the middle of the rope. Hold the handles of the rope in each hand and pull the rope up tight. The handles should come up to the upper chest level. If the rope measures below the chest, use a longer rope. If it measures above the chest use a shorter rope. Beaded ropes can easily be adjusted for your height.

Proper Form

If you are just a beginner to jump roping or you are performing an assortment of masterful foot patterns, follow the basic rules below.

- Jump slightly off the floor, only an inch or two, keeping the knees slightly bent.
- Land on the floor softly, rolling through the balls of the feet.
- Ensure shoulders are down and relaxed.
- Keep the neck relaxed and the head in a neutral position.
- Jump with the body upright. Do not lean forward or backward.
- Start turning the rope with the wrists and forearms, with limited movement at the shoulders.
- Keep the arms close to the sides of the body. Make sure the arms do not move away from the body. If the arms are raised there is less rope length to jump through and this may lead to the rope getting tangled in the feet and tripping.
- Wear cross-trainers. The feet require support and padding when jumping for an extended amount of time.
- Aim for a pace of 120–160 jumps per minute.
- Never sacrifice good jumping form for speed.

Neutral Moves

Jumping rope can be challenging to even the most seasoned athlete. One of the more difficult challenges in jumping rope is to keep going and not give up. The use of neutral and resting moves can be incorporated to help beginners improve their conditioning.

To execute a neutral move, put both handles in one hand and turn the rope in a forward motion, to the side of the body, as you continue jumping. Do not allow the rope to wander in front of your body. Keep it to your sides. Occasionally change the rope to the opposite hand to add variety, and to become comfortable with different arm positions. Performing a basic jog or march, while continually turning the rope, will keep the heart rate elevated and may reduce the frustration of stopping and starting. Accomplished jump ropers use neutral moves to add variety to their workout, allowing for higher training intensities. Once your conditioning has improved, you will be able to jump rope continually.

Two-Step Breakdown

The two-step breakdown is a systematic training method which divides up more complicated moves into manageable elements. The moves can then be easily practised and learned. In the first step, both handles of the rope are placed into one hand and the new move is executed while turning the rope to one side, much like the neutral or resting moves. Change the handles to the other hand and practise the move again. Once you feel comfortable with your timing, progress to the second step and attempt to perform the move jumping through the rope.

Step 1   Grab both handles in one hand, turning it to the side of the body (a neutral or resting move), and practise your new move or combination.
Step 2   Hold the rope handles in each hand and try the movement jumping through the rope.

When you are ready to take on more challenging jumps, the two-step breakdown will help you succeed.

Mastering jump rope does take practice, but there are rewards. Within a few weeks you will be putting together foot and arm combinations that will improve your agility, balance and physical conditioning.

Jumps and Combinations

There are hundreds of different jump rope combinations, including numerous arm and foot patterns. Here are a series of jumps with difficulty level ranging from beginner to advanced.

The Basic Double-Foot Jump (difficulty level 1)

Hold the handles comfortably in the hands, keep the arms by the sides of the body and both feet side by side. Push off the floor into the air while rotating the rope upward behind the back, over the head, in front of the body, and under the feet. Roll through the balls of the feet when landing, keeping the knees slightly bent in order to absorb impact. The arms stay by the side of the body and rotate the rope with the wrists. Do not push up too high as beginners have a tendency to over-jump.

Basic double-foot jump.

Boxer's Skip (difficulty level 1)

As you jump, shift your weight from one foot to the other maintaining a smooth rhythm. Keep the knees slightly bent as you switch from one foot to the other. Make sure you are not jumping too high and your shoulders and neck remain relaxed. Vary the footwork, for example singles (side-to-side) or doubles (double right, double left). Repeat.

Jump Kicks (difficulty level 2)

Perform a basic two-foot jump. While jumping on one foot lift the other foot slightly backward and then kick it forward. Repeat the two-foot jump again and repeat the kick with the other foot. Travel to the front and back.

RIGHT: Boxer's skip.

Jump kick, lifting the foot back.

Jump kick, kicking the foot front.

Toe taps.

Tap with alternate foot.

Toe Taps (difficulty level 2)

Start from the double-foot jump and bring one foot forward, tapping the toe on the floor in front. Alternate this front toe tap with both feet, smoothly shifting your weight from foot to foot.

Slalom (difficulty level 2)

Jump from side to side with a skiing motion, keeping the ankles together. Start jumping slightly side-to-side and increase the distance as you become more comfortable with the movement. Often with side-to-side movements the arms have a tendency to travel outward, which could cause the rope to catch the feet. Hold the arms by the sides of the body and use the wrist as the pivot point.

Slalom left.

Slalom right.

Reverse Jump (difficulty level 3)

Rotate the rope in a backward direction as you jump. The challenge is to maintain proper hand and arm position, as there is a tendency to raise the arms to lift the rope over the head.

High Knee Lifts (difficulty level 3)

This move is similar to jogging on the spot, but with a rope. Pull your abdominal muscles in tight as you lift your knees up high in front. Lift the knees as high as possible, concentrating on the push-off phase of one foot, then the other foot. The body stays upright and the hands and arms by the sides of the body. Land softly, absorbing some of the impact through the legs. Repeat ten to twenty high knee lifts and then recover by performing the boxer's skip. To decrease intensity, add a hop in between the knee lifts.

LEFT: Reverse jump.

BELOW LEFT: High knee lifts.

BELOW RIGHT: Lift your knees high in front.

Jumping jacks, feet apart.

Jumping jacks, feet together.

Jumping Jacks (difficulty level 3)

As you jump, separate the feet about shoulder-width apart, landing softly through the feet. Jump and bring the feet together before landing on the floor. Try not to separate the feet too wide as they will get entangled in the rope.

Combo Jump 1: Jumping Jack–Knee Lift (difficulty level 3)

This combination move starts with performing one jumping jack, followed by lifting one knee. A basic jump or hop allows you to transition from the jumping jack to the high knee lift. Perform another jumping jack and finish with lifting the other knee.

Combo jump 1, jumping jack.

Add high knee lift.

Ali shuffle, alternating feet front and back.

Ali Shuffle (difficulty level 3)

Muhammad Ali was known for his fast footwork. In the ring Ali would suddenly shuffle his feet front and back to distract his opponents. The Ali shuffle is similar to the toe tap jumps, but the movement is exaggerated slightly. Push off both feet equally, with the body weight centred over the feet, and land on the balls of the feet, alternating the feet front and back. The centre of gravity changes slightly when both feet change position, and this forward and backward movement develops foot agility and reaction time. Land softly and move quickly.

Push off both feet equally.

Land on the balls of the feet and shuffle quickly.

Combo jump 2, Ali shuffle.

Smoothly transition to jumping jack.

Combo Jump 2: Ali Shuffle and Jumping Jacks (difficulty level 4)

Combining the Ali shuffle with jumping jacks helps to improve balance, timing and agility. Begin with eight shuffles, then eight jacks. In order to transition from the shuffle to the jack, perform a basic two-foot jump: Shuffle–shuffle–basic jump–jack. Decrease down to a single shuffle, basic jump and a single jack. Repeat.

Scissors (difficulty level 4)

Add leg crossovers to the jumping jack. Jump and land on the floor with the legs about shoulder-width apart. Jump bringing the legs in and crossing them in the air. Land on the floor with the feet crossed. Repeat jumping with the feet in a wide position. Bring the feet back to centre ensuring you alternate the foot position when performing the scissor move.

Scissors start with jumping jack.

Scissor crossover.

Diamond jump.

Diamond Jump (difficulty level 4)

Perform a single jump at each point of an imaginary diamond. With both feet together, push off, moving six to eight inches to any point. Change direction and repeat the jumps. The quick change in direction is a great way to improve agility and leg power.

Double Under (difficulty level 5)

For this challenging jump, the rope travels twice under the jumper while in the air. Start with eight to ten double jumps and then the boxer's skip. Increase the number of jumps per session, interspersed with the boxer's skip, working up to three or four sets of twenty double jumps. This demanding jump requires strong legs and good anaerobic fitness. Remember: two fast rotations of the rope with the one higher jump performed.

Double under.

Crossovers: cross the arms in front of the body.

Crossovers (difficulty level 5)

Performing the basic double foot jump, cross the rope in front of the body on the first jump and then uncross the arms on the second jump. Ensure the hands are kept at hip level with the rope handles pointing out to the sides and not down toward the floor. You will have a dominant side and therefore a tendency to cross the same arm in front or back each time. Once you master the jump, change the position of the arms with each crossover: right arm in front of left arm, and left arm in front of right arm. Work up to performing continuous crossovers, travelling forward and backward.

Jump through the rope.

Uncross the arms.

Figure eight, rope on one side of the body.

Figure Eight Jump (difficulty level 5)

Basically this is one figure eight movement of the rope and one basic double foot jump. With the wrists together and elbows tight to the body, rotate the rope in a figure eight from one side to the other in front of the body. As the rope comes back to centre open the hands and jump through the rope performing one basic double foot jump. The key is to allow the hands to uncross and open them wide. For a real challenge, perform this jump faster, lowering the centre jump toward the floor (side-side-centre).

Incorporate a wide variety of jumps and combinations into your training routine. Take the time to learn the basic jumps and commit to working on dynamic foot movement.

Rotate the rope on the other side of the body.

Jump through the rope.

A wood-sprung floor is the best surface to jump rope on.

Amir Khan training.

Freeform Jumping

Jump rope should never become stale or boring. Be creative and always challenge yourself. There are hundreds of different skipping patterns and they all start with the basics. Once you master the basic jumps incorporate more intricate jumps into your training. Vary the speed, tempo and selection, perform double jumps, jumping jacks, combination jumps and sprints, and increase your pace, incorporating complex footwork.

COMMON ERRORS AND QUICK FIXES

Error: The rope gets caught on the feet.

Quick fix: This often occurs when the arms are held too wide. Keep the elbows tucked in and the hands by the hips. Rotate the rope with your wrists and forearms in a smooth movement, keeping the shoulders steady and relaxed. Look straight forward and not down at your feet.

Error: Jumping in one place. Nothing stays still in the ring, so why jump in one place?

Quick fix: Travel forward, backward and side-to-side, preparing yourself for movement in the ring.

Error: Difficulty learning new jumps.

Quick fix: Everything starts with the basics, so get them right first. Practise more complicated jumps without using the rope. Add the rope once you are more comfortable with the new move. Jumping rope in front of a mirror is also a great way to observe your form and make adjustments.

Error: Double hopping.

Quick fix: This generally occurs with beginners, when a few quick little hops are performed just after the rope passes under the feet. It is a difficult habit to break. Jump only once for every revolution of the rope, in order to be efficient and not waste energy. It sometimes helps to increase your rope speed.

Jump rope places demands on every muscle in your body.

CHAPTER 6

ROADWORK

A successful boxer's training regimen needs to include all aspects of physical training, such as muscular strength and endurance, flexibility, technical skills, agility, power, balance and cardio-conditioning. Effective roadwork improves the ability of the heart and lungs to adapt to the demands placed on the body during physical training. Roadwork develops the cardio-respiratory and vascular systems so you can 'go the distance' in a boxing match.

When old-school coaches talk about roadwork they are referring to a three- to ten-kilometre (two- to six-mile) run. These runs play an important role in

a boxer's training, but there are more effective ways to prepare for battle in the ring. Due to the explosive nature of boxing, faster paced, higher intensity sprints also need to be included in your training. Imitating the demands of multiple three-minute rounds is essential and this is accomplished by performing running sprints and interval training. An intense fight requires an increased amount of oxygen to be delivered to the working muscles.

Will roadwork get your body ready for the demands associated with a gruelling sparring session or match? The answer is 'no'. However, an intelligent roadwork/running programme will enhance the conditioning that you get from working various bags, focus mitts and sparring. If you have two equally skilled boxers, the boxer who includes roadwork as part of a well-thought-out training plan will more often than not be the victorious boxer.

Even though fights are won by throwing punches, it is your legs that get you in and out of range. Getting into position to land a punch or moving to evade an opponent's punches is almost impossible if your legs are not in top shape. Roadwork builds endurance and promotes explosiveness in the ring. Manny Pacquiao is constantly moving when he is in the ring, pivoting, springing forward, backward and dipping. Muhammad Ali, Sugar Ray Leonard, Roy Jones Jr and Juan Manuel Márquez are examples of great 'movers' in the ring.

Roadwork.

Considerations

Footwear

Purchase a comfortable and functional pair of running shoes. When your foot strikes the ground the force produced is many times that of your body weight, so ensure that the shoes have good heel support, sole cushioning and mid-sole flexibility. Consider your body type, foot structure and where you will be running to assist in determining your shoe choice. Visit a store that has a knowledgeable and trained staff and try on many different styles before making an educated purchase.

Hot Weather

It generally takes a few weeks for your body to adjust to a large increase in temperature so reduce the intensity of training in hot and humid weather. Run during the coolest part of the day – early morning or in the evening – and stay out of direct sunlight.

Wear light-coloured breathable fabrics that fit to allow for free and comfortable movement. Clothing is now made with moisture-transport capabilities that allow perspiration to evaporate away from the body, and with UV protection built into the fabric. Protect your eyes from UV rays with non-slip sunglasses and wear a hat or bandana for cooling and UV protection benefits.

Ensure you are well hydrated by consuming water before, during and after exercise. An active person should drink two to three litres (3½ pints or 8 cups to 5 pints or 12 cups) of water a day. When running, drink four to six ounces (110g or ½ cup to 170g or ¾ cup) of fluid at twenty-minute intervals. Alcohol, tea, coffee and colas act as diuretics and can actually increase fluid loss so it is best to avoid these drinks. Sports drinks that replenish the electrolyte balance in your body may be a good choice when running for an extended period of time (more than one hour) and if it is extremely hot.

Stay hydrated when running in the heat.

Cold Weather

Do not train outside on extremely windy and icy days, or if the temperature is below −10°C (15°F). To improve your footing on slippery roads, shorten your stride length, placing the foot on the ground and then lifting the foot during the push-off phase.

When running in cold weather, always dress in layers, and ensure the head and hands are covered and the face is protected. Start with a wicking base layer to keep your body dry and warm. Then layer with an insulating material, such as fleece. This layer assists with the wicking of moisture and also traps air close to the body to keep you warm. The third outer layer should be of wind-resistant and water-proof material to protect against the wind and wet weather. Fifty per cent of the body's heat is lost through the head, and even more through the hands if they are not covered. Wear a toque or balaclava on your head, gloves or mitts on your hands, and a covering over your mouth and nose to warm the air you are breathing. If the sun is shining wear sunscreen and high-quality UV sunglasses to protect your eyes.

Meals

It is best to wait at least ninety minutes after eating a full meal before training, and the larger the meal the longer you should wait before a long run. Working out too soon after a large meal may cause an ineffective workout as the body is expending resources digesting food and not providing oxygen to the working muscles.

Illness

Following an illness (e.g. flu or a respiratory infection) it is best to rest until you have felt well for a full twenty-four hours. Following an illness it can take several weeks to regain strength, so it is important to adjust your training when you start back. If you are taking prescription or over-the-counter medications, always consult with your doctor or medical professional before returning to your training programme.

Pollution

If the pollution index is high, it may be best to train indoors to reduce the occurrence of respiratory issues.

Effective Running Technique

For a more successful running session and to help reduce the chance of injuries, start with the correct form and running technique.

- Look straight ahead, chin and head in a neutral position.
- Keep your shoulders relaxed.
- Keep your elbows bent at 90 degrees, letting the arms swing naturally forward and backward.
- Keep the fists relaxed and the hands partly open.
- Hold the body core muscles tight for back support and the hips with a slight tip upward.
- Avoid moving the knees up and down excessively. Move the knees in a smooth horizontal motion.
- Allow the foot to swing forward naturally, landing with the foot in front of the knee.
- Aim for a quick foot turnover, reducing the amount of contact time with the ground.
- Maintain a comfortable running style.

Relaxed arm swing.

Move the knees in a smooth horizontal motion.

Training Intensities

The 'Talk Test' Measure of Exercise Intensity

The talk test allows you to judge your ability to talk while working out. Measuring how easy or difficult it is to talk while you are exercising will give you an indicator of how hard you are training. Generally, if you are working at a lower to moderate intensity level you are able to talk comfortably. When you are working at a more intense level you will feel breathless and will draw in deep breaths of air. During long runs you should be working at a moderate intensity. When performing sprints and intervals you should work at an intense level where it will be more difficult to talk.

The Training Heart Rate

Your goal, whether warming up, working aerobically during long runs, or challenging yourself when sprinting, is to work within your training heart rate zone. To obtain your maximum heart rate the age-predicted maximum heart rate formula (Karvonen) is used. Two hundred and twenty minus your age will give your maximum heart rate number. Multiply this number by the percentage you want to work at and use the resulting number to monitor your workout.

Determining your working heart rate will help you monitor if you are in your training heart rate zone. During a workout session periodically stop exercising and immediately take your pulse, counting for fifteen seconds. Multiply this number by four to obtain your working heart rate. For a more accurate measure of your exercising heart rate use a heart rate monitor. These portable devices allow you to record your heart rate without stopping your workout.

Carotid pulse: place the index finger on the side of the neck and find the pulse. Press lightly.

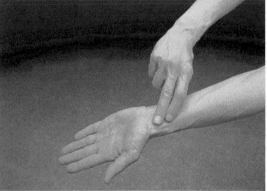

Radial pulse: find your pulse by placing your index finger on the inside of the wrist.

For a quick reference with respect to your age, training intensity and beats per minute (bpm), refer to the table below.

Roadwork Training

As mentioned previously, old-school boxers would train by going out for long runs. They also had to complete fifteen rounds. Today the championship distance is twelve rounds; pro fighters start with four rounds and eventually work their way up to ten-round fights. Whether your goal is to be a professional fighter or an amateur fighter, your legs have to be in top shape. Long runs develop the groundwork to build your stamina for a match. The goal is to perform this aerobic activity for between twenty and sixty minutes. Longer distance runs also help you make weight for an approaching match. As your distances increase and your conditioning improves, interval work and sprints need to be worked into your training. Depending on your current physical condition, you may want to follow the walk/run programme, then progress to longer runs and add interval/sprint training.

Sample running sessions are given below. Pick the one best suited to your current fitness level.

Warm-Up

It is important to warm up before you start your roadwork. A great way to increase the blood flow in the body is to warm up by shadowboxing, moving side-to-side, and forward and backward, and throwing punches for a few minutes. You can also warm up by walking at a brisk pace for five minutes. Once you are warmed up, perform some pre-activity stretches.

Warm up by shadowboxing.

Heart Rate Training Intensities (bpm)							
Age (years)	50%	60%	65%	70%	75%	80%	90%
18	136	149	156	162	169	176	189
20	135	148	155	161	168	174	187
25	133	145	151	158	164	170	183
30	130	142	148	154	160	166	178
35	128	139	145	151	156	162	174
40	125	136	142	147	153	158	169
45	123	133	138	144	149	154	165
50	120	130	135	140	145	150	160
55	118	127	132	137	141	146	156
60	115	124	129	133	138	142	151
65	113	121	125	130	134	138	147
70	110	118	122	126	130	134	142

Based on a resting heart rate of seventy beats per minute.

The Walk–Run Method
(level 1: just starting out)

By alternating between walking and running, varying the times and/or distances of your walk/run, you will start to build strength, stamina and endurance. Before long you will be running longer and farther. This method of training also reduces the chances of overuse injuries to the muscles and the joints.

Start by walking briskly for three minutes followed by running for three minutes. Work up to six-minute running intervals, decreasing your walking time. Continue to alternate the walk and run for twelve to fifteen minutes, increasing to a total time of thirty to forty-five minutes. Work at sixty to seventy per cent of your maximum heart rate. Decrease your walk time and increase your run time. Once you are able to run continuously for twenty minutes (this often takes four to six weeks), you are ready to take it up a notch.

Long Roadwork Runs (level 2)

Start by running for a continuous twenty-minute period and gradually increase your distance and time. Ensure that every week or two you add one half to one kilometre to your run. Always work within your training heart rate zone, starting with sixty to seventy per cent of your maximum heart rate and working up to seventy to eighty per cent of your maximum heart rate. After you are able to run comfortably for forty-five to sixty minutes, increase your pace slightly by increasing your training heart rate. The long runs will build your cardiovascular conditioning and endurance, as well as improve your leg strength and endurance.

Once you have mastered long runs, it is time to include intervals into your training.

High Intensity Interval Training (level 3)

Adding interval drills to your roadwork offers a challenging and rewarding session to your roadwork training that builds strength, speed and endurance. In order to reduce the risk of injury, ensure you are in good physical condition before including intervals in your training. Modify the sprint intervals according

Interval training.

to your current physical condition and the goals you have set for yourself.

Timed sprints

For the conditioned athlete, interval training challenges and trains the body by placing intense demands on the cardiovascular system and the muscles for a time lapse of fifteen to thirty seconds. Including interval training into your roadwork will improve your anaerobic power, speed and belief in yourself. You will learn to sustain the higher level of effort to complete the work and it is this higher level of effort that is often required to endure multiple high intensity three-minute rounds.

Run hard for a shorter period, working anywhere from seventy-five to ninety per cent of your maximum heart rate. You will definitely feel out of your comfort zone. Allow your heart rate to lower to sixty-five to seventy-five per cent during the rest periods. Keep your interval speed work to only ten per cent of your weekly roadwork and the sessions need only last for about thirty minutes.

Keep your running intervals short so you become familiar with how it feels to push yourself. With the intense demands of interval training, the muscles must react faster and become familiar with the quick movements. There is a greater chance of muscle strains and pulls. When performing sprints, lactic acid is produced from the intense physical demands. This often causes cramping and discomfort in the muscles and may result in making you want to quit. Keep your training heart rate around eighty-five per cent, with your effort at 100 to 110 per cent.

Begin your interval training sessions with an easy to moderate pace, running for five minutes. In the next five minutes gradually increase your pace to the moderate level, increasing the heart rate and warming up the muscles. Next sprint as fast as you can for fifteen to thirty seconds. Reduce your speed to a comfortable pace to recover. Recovery takes anywhere from one to four minutes depending on your fitness level. The better physical condition you are in, the less time it will take you to recover. You are ready to sprint again when your target heart rate is at sixty to seventy per cent. Repeat the sprints and recovery phase for three to six cycles. Cool down at an easy pace for five to ten minutes.

Track sprints

Performing interval training on a track allows you to measure off and run specific distances. Gradually warm up for five to ten minutes by running at an easy pace, including some light stretches. Start your first sprint at moderate intensity, gradually increasing to near maximum speed. Sprinting distances are between 100 and 400 metres (110–440 yards), working at seventy-five to ninety per cent of your maximum heart rate. Recover by running at a moderate pace for 400–800 metres (440–880 yards). Repeat this sequence six to eight times. After your final sprint, run slowly for five minutes to lower your heart rate and recover.

To produce the greatest running speed, push off the ground forcefully, bringing the leg fully forward and then pulling it down and backward as the foot makes contact with the track. Keep the leg movement smooth, body tall, and breathe deep into the abdomen.

Track sprints.

Hill sprints

Adding hill sprints to your roadwork training allows you to train at a higher intensity. The inclined surface forces you to lean forward and use the proper leg mechanics for a quick acceleration on a flat surface. Your arm movement at the shoulders is forceful and deliberate, developing upper body drive. When running up an inclined surface it is difficult to reach maximum limb speed and the powerful push from the hamstring muscles and calf muscles is reduced. This will reduce the risk of muscle injuries. Hill sprints challenge and strengthen the lower back, gluteals, hamstrings and calf muscles. The hill also challenges your psyche. Once you start your drive up the hill, use the momentum to get to the top and be victorious.

Start with an easy warm-up, running on a flat surface for five to ten minutes. Then loosen up the hip area, knees, ankles and shoulders with hip and ankle rotations, shoulder shrugs and dynamic stretches for the legs. Prepare for your hill sprints by performing three to five hill runs working at sixty-five to eighty per cent of your maximum heart rate.

Listed below are some shorter distance sprints which will reduce the risk of stress on the muscles, while still challenging your cardiovascular system. The rest periods increase as the sprint time increases to ensure you are recovered sufficiently to perform the next sprint with an effective technique. Perform the following sprints at eighty-five to ninety per cent of your maximum heart rate.

5 × 9 metres (10 yards) (rest 30 seconds in between)
4 × 18 metres (20 yards) (rest 40 seconds in between)
3 × 27 metres (30 yards) (rest 60 seconds in between)
2 × 36 metres (40 yards) (rest 90 seconds in between)
1 × 46+ metres (50+ yards) if the hill is long enough

If you have longer hills (180–360m; 200–400 yards) with a good incline to train on, incorporate some longer hill training into your roadwork. Warm up with an easy run for five to ten minutes and perform an easy stretch. Then start your hill training, attacking the hill fast enough that you are working at seventy-five to eighty-five per cent of your maximum heart rate, pacing yourself to be able to reach the top. Once you reach the top, use the walk down to the bottom of the hill to recover. Start with four hill repeats, working up to ten to twelve repeats.

Whether running or sprinting up a hill, lean the body slightly into the hill, pumping your arms in a forward, backward movement, and lifting your knees high with rapid foot turnover. Keep the movement pushing forward and your effort consistent.

Uphill Technique
- Shorten your stride length, with the arms and legs synchronized.
- Keep the chest up and momentum forward as you lean into the hill.
- Keep the body weight forward onto the balls of the feet.

Hill sprints.

Uphill technique.

- Increase your effort as you run past the top of the hill.

Downhill Technique
- Open your stride and keep your core muscles engaged.
- Maintain control as you let gravity pull you along.
- Concentrate on the running surface, watching for loose stones and slippery conditions.
- Maintain the proper foot placement and arm swing.

Interval training, sprints and hill runs cannot be performed every day. The body needs time to recover and a lower intensity distance run is a good alternative which allows you to continue training.

BELOW LEFT: Downhill technique.
BELOW RIGHT: Distance runs.

The Importance of Stretching

Include stretching exercises in your workouts on a regular basis to improve your overall flexibility and range of motion. Stretching reduces the chance of muscle pulls or strains and assists in obtaining an optimal range of motion at a joint and within a muscle. The flexibility at a joint is influenced by the length and suppleness of the muscle, the length and insertion of the ligaments and tendons, the bone shape and the cartilage placement. Genetics does partially determine the flexibility of your joints, but it can be improved and enhanced by performing stretching exercises on a regular basis.

Boxers need to have flexible muscles and good mobility in the shoulders, upper body and legs to provide the opportunity to produce the best possible athletic outcome. The key is to have the correct flexibility for your sport, allowing sufficient movement through a desired range that does not strain the muscles or impinge the joint.

To improve your flexibility, perform a variety of stretching exercises. Always warm up the muscles and the joint area before you start any stretching exercises. Perform gentle rotations in both directions at all the joints, working from head to toe. Warm up the circulatory system by bouncing around, jogging slowly or easy shadowboxing.

A static stretch is the safest way to stretch. The muscle is lengthened slightly beyond its normal length and to a point of mild discomfort. Hold the stretch for fifteen to sixty seconds and repeat two to three times. Do not force the stretch or over-stretch the muscle, as this will cause muscle strain and pain.

Dynamic stretching is another way to increase the length of the muscle and increase the joint range of motion. Dynamic stretching involves performing a controlled swinging motion of a limb to gradually increase the joint mobility and muscle length. Movement of the muscle occurs during the stretch but, unlike the static stretch, it is not held. Repeat the movement ten to fifteen times. Controlled arm swing, torso twists and legs swings are examples of dynamic stretching.

Bouncing or ballistic stretching uses momentum to force a joint beyond its normal range of motion. The muscles, tendons or ligaments can be easily

The key is to have the correct flexibility for your sport.

overstretched by ballistic stretching and it is never recommended because of the high incidence of injury.

It is important to perform a brief stretch before a workout, and after warming up. Take the muscles and joints through the full range of motion by imitating the actions of boxing. This is usually a dynamic stretching movement and will continue to increase the blood flow to the working muscles. Reduce muscle tightness by holding the stretch for ten to fifteen seconds.

The post-activity stretch assists in lengthening the working muscle back to its initial length. After activity the muscles and joints are warmed, and this is the best time to work on improving your flexibility and lengthening the muscle. Slow static stretching assists in reducing the soreness of localized muscles brought on by repetitive movements. Hold the post-activity stretch for at least twenty seconds up to sixty seconds, at the point where mild tension is felt. Relax and then reset the stretch by moving further into it.

It is imperative to stretch after your workout. Boxing workouts can be gruelling and the muscles and joints undergo constant movement as the result of numerous repetitions of jabs, straight rights, hooks and uppercuts. Poor flexibility can lead to injuries, pain and discomfort, especially at the shoulders. Working on specific movements with your legs and feet and moving on your toes, whether it is jumping rope or in the ring, places stress on the leg muscles and joints and these sport-specific demands can cause the muscle to become very tight and inflexible. By performing post-activity stretches, the muscle tissue is lengthened to give the proper alignment of the muscles and joints. Work towards an optimal range of motion and being able to move from a flexed position to an extended position. Having an optimum range of motion and flexibility reduces the risk of injury and allows for improved performance.

Stretching Exercises

Before starting your workout move the limbs and muscles through an optimal range of motion with little to no tension on the muscle or joints, and hold the stretches for ten to fifteen seconds. After your workout, perform the stretches for a longer period of time, holding them for twenty to sixty seconds. Breathe in as you prepare for the stretch and breathe out slowly as you go into the stretch. Find the point where there is a gentle tension on the muscle and hold the stretch until this mild tension disappears and the muscle starts to relax. Stretch both sides of the body uniformly. Remember to focus on stretching the muscle and not placing any stress on the joints.

Upper back stretch
Hold the hands together with arms extended in front of the body. Reach forward at the shoulders, pressing the palms of the hands away from the body. Relax and round through the upper back. Hold the stretch and then repeat.

Chest and shoulder stretch
Stand with your arms behind your back, hands held

Upper back stretch.

Chest and shoulder stretch.

together and fingers interlaced. Straighten your arms, lifting them up slightly behind the body and at the same time pull your shoulder blades together. Ensure that you are looking forward and the neck muscles are relaxed. This exercise will stretch the shoulder muscles, chest area and the arms. Hold until you feel the muscles relaxing and lengthening.

Centre back and shoulder stretch

To stretch the centre of the upper back, extend a straight arm fully across the chest, holding on to the elbow area with the other hand, and press gently toward the opposite shoulder. Release the press. Now bend the arm at the elbow and press across the chest toward the opposite shoulder in order to stretch the shoulder region. Hold the stretches and repeat on both sides.

BELOW LEFT: Centre back stretch.
BELOW RIGHT: Shoulder stretch.

Triceps stretch.

Standing quadriceps/hip flexor stretch.

Triceps stretch
With both of your arms up over your head, point one elbow up toward the ceiling. Hold this elbow with the opposite hand and press down toward the centre of the back until you feel a slight tension in the triceps muscle. Hold the stretch and repeat with the other elbow pointing toward the ceiling.

Standing quadriceps/hip flexor stretch
To stretch the quadriceps muscle at the front of the thigh, stand tall on one leg and bend the other leg, lifting the heel up toward the buttock. Keep the knees fairly close together. In order to stretch the hip flexor muscle, stay in the same position with knees together and press the hips forward, allowing the supporting leg to bend at the knee slightly. Repeat this stretch on both sides and until the muscle has relaxed and lengthened.

Standing calf/Achilles stretch
Stand with both feet facing straight forward; step forward with one leg, bending at the knee. The back leg is extended long and the heel of the back foot stays on the floor. The body weight is held over the front leg. The stretch should be felt in the centre of the calf muscle of the back leg. If you bend the back leg slightly and transfer some of your body weight toward the back heel, the lower portion of the calf and the Achilles tendon will be stretched. Repeat this stretch on both sides.

Seated hamstring stretch
Sit on the floor with one leg extended long, foot flexed and the other leg bent in toward the body. Bend the body forward from the hips over the extended leg, keeping the back as flat and long as possible. Stretch forward slowly and only to the point where you feel the stretch or tension at the back of the extended leg. Repeat with both legs.

Standing calf/Achilles stretch.

RIGHT: *Seated hamstring stretch.*
BELOW LEFT: *Supine hamstring stretch.*
BELOW RIGHT: *Seated hip stretch.*

Supine hamstring stretch

To stretch the hamstring muscle, lie on your back with one leg bent, foot on the floor, and the other leg extended up over the body. With both hands pull the extended leg slowly back toward the chest until you feel the tension in the hamstring muscle. Hold until the muscle relaxes and lengthens. Repeat on both sides.

Seated hip stretch

To stretch the gluteus muscles and increase mobility in the hip region, sit on the floor, one leg extended long in front of you and the other leg crossed over with the foot on the floor. Rotate the upper body so the opposite shoulder is close to the knee and the head turned looking over the back shoulder. Hold this rotation until the muscle relaxes, release and repeat on the other side.

CHAPTER 7

STRENGTH TRAINING

Strength training increases overall stamina, punching power, foot speed and lean body mass. Professional boxers such as Manny Pacquiao, Sergio Martinez and Floyd Mayweather Jr believe that strength training is essential to the whole training package, complementing their overall outcome.

The emphasis of a strength training programme is to supplement your boxing programme, and develop muscular strength and endurance. This provides the basis for stronger and more powerful punches, allowing for improvements in speed, agility and response time. Strength training gets you ready for the battle in the ring.

The Medicine Ball

It does not get more 'old school' than training with a medicine ball, which is a staple part of a boxer's training regimen. Successful boxers know that well-armoured abdominal muscles are essential as protection against body attacks.

Strength training using the medicine ball.

The invention of the medicine ball dates back to around 400 BC when the ancient Greek physicians used sand-filled animal skin pouches to help patients recover from injuries. Medicine balls come in different types and sizes. Traditionally made from leather, they are now made from various materials (such as vinyl, rubber and neoprene) and are filled with sand, steel shot, or gel-filled polyvinyl chloride shells. Ranging in weight from 1kg to 14kg (2–30lb), the medicine ball delivers an incredibly effective workout, not only for the core muscles but also for the entire body.

The medicine ball allows for a greater range of motion at the joint areas than working with weights and is one of the most versatile strength training tools. Due to the resiliency of the ball, not only can it be lifted, pushed and pressed, it also has dynamic movement when it is thrown or tossed. In doing so, reaction time and alertness are challenged and agility is developed.

Core Strength Exercises

Medicine Ball Crunch

While holding the medicine ball against your chest and keeping your back and feet on the floor, raise the upper body and head off the floor. Aim to touch the ball against your thighs. Slowly curl back to the floor. Repeat the basic curl-up for three sets, ten to twenty repetitions with a 3–5kg (6–12lb) medicine ball.

Medicine ball crunch.

Overhead Pull-Up

Start by lying flat on the floor with the arms extended overhead and hold the ball firmly between the hands. Keep the arms extended and hold the ball as you sit up. Return to your start position on the floor, lowering the head, shoulders and ball in unison. Perform one to three sets of ten to fifteen repetitions with a 3–5kg (6–10lb) medicine ball.

Overhead pull-up: start.

Overhead pull-up: finish.

Seated ball crunch: start.

Seated ball crunch: finish.

Seated Ball Crunch

Sitting in an upright position, lean back on your hands with the elbows slightly bent. Place the medicine ball between the knees and squeeze it tight. Now pull the knees and ball toward your chest. Lower the feet toward the floor. Perform one to three sets of ten to fifteen repetitions with a 3–5kg (6–10lb) medicine ball.

Side Pullover Sit-Up

Start by lying flat on the floor and hold the medicine ball over the right shoulder. The ball is resting on the floor. Sit up as you pull the ball across to the opposite knee in a smooth arc. Slowly lower to the start position. Repeat the workout on one side completely before performing on the other side. Perform one to two sets of ten to fifteen repetitions with a 3–5kg (6–10lb) medicine ball.

Side pullover sit-up: start.

Side pullover sit-up: finish.

V-ups: start.

V-ups: double legs.

V-ups: single leg.

V-Ups

Begin V-ups by lying flat on the floor, with the legs extended and the arms straight overhead holding the medicine ball. Lift the legs, body and arms simultaneously until you reach a V position with the body and the legs. Reach the ball toward the feet, aiming to touch the feet. Hold the V and then lower the body and legs together back to the floor. Ensure the movement is smooth and in control with the legs held together and the arms straight throughout the exercise. If you are unable to lift both legs together, perform a single leg V-up. A single leg lift is slightly easier on the lower back muscles. One leg remains straight on the floor while you lift the other leg at the same time as the body and arms are raised. Reach the ball toward the feet. Perform two to three sets of ten to fifteen repetitions with a 3–4kg (6–8lb) medicine ball.

Stay close to your partner.

After a series of passes, change direction.

Back-to-Back Ball Pass (partner drill)

Start this exercise standing back to back with your partner. Hold the ball at chest level, twisting the body to the right and pass the ball to your partner. Your partner twists to their left to receive the ball and then twists to the right to pass the ball as you twist to your left to receive the ball. This is one repetition. Keep both feet on the floor and ensure the twist is the result of a good rotation through the body. Change direction once you have completed the desired number of repetitions. This exercise helps to strengthen the oblique abdominal muscles and the lower back muscles. Perform one to three sets of fifteen to twenty repetitions with a 4–5kg (8–10lb) medicine ball.

Partner Toss (partner drill)

Sit facing your partner at a distance of three to four feet (1–1.5m). One partner holds the ball at chest level. Each partner performs a sit-up at the same time, one with the ball, one without the ball. As

Partner toss: start.

Toss the ball as you sit up.

you sit up, toss the ball to your partner. When the ball is caught, return slowly toward the floor, keeping the ball close to the chest and repeat. Always ensure your partner has their arms ready to catch the ball and the timing is synchronized. Perform two to three sets of twelve to fifteen tosses (count one repetition each time you toss the ball). Rest in between the sets and use a 3–5kg (6–10lb) medicine ball.

Lower Body Drills

Forward Lunges

Stand holding the ball at chest level with the feet together. With the core muscles held tight, lift one foot off the floor and balance on the standing foot. Stay in this balanced position and then step forward, placing the heel of the foot on the floor first, and then shift the body weight to the full foot. Do not allow the body to tilt or sway to one side, or the front knee to bend past ninety degrees. Lower the body until the thigh of the front leg is parallel with the floor. The back leg bends, acting as a stabilizer. There is a slight forward bend at the hips and the back remains straight. Push off the front leg firmly and return to the start position. Repeat the step forward with the other leg. This counts as one repetition. Perform two to three sets of ten to fifteen repetitions with a 5–10kg (10–20lb) ball.

CENTRE RIGHT: Forward lunge: ready position.
RIGHT: Forward lunge: step forward.

Overhead squats.

Overhead squats: raising medicine ball overhead.

Overhead Squats

Hold the ball at waist level, standing with the feet shoulder-width apart. Raise the ball overhead as you bend the knees into a squat position. Hold the core muscles tight with the back straight, sitting back with the body weight over the heels. Hold the squat and the arms overhead for two seconds and then lower the ball and straighten the legs to the starting position. Perform two to three sets of twenty to twenty-five repetitions with a 5–10kg (12–25lb) medicine ball.

Power Jump Squats (advanced)

Hold the ball at chest level and feet shoulder-width apart. Lower down into a squat, pause and then use explosive power to push up into the air as high as

possible. Roll through the balls of your feet in a controlled landing, lowering all the way through into a squat position. Pause before you jump again. Perform two to three sets of ten to fifteen repetitions with a 5–12kg (10–25lb) ball.

Upper Body Drills

Off-Set Push-Ups (advanced)

Place one hand on the ball and the other hand on the floor in a push-up position. Legs are extended long and straight, with the balls of the feet on the floor. The medicine ball provides an unsteady hand placement position, which makes this push-up very challenging. The shoulder muscles work harder to

Power jump squats: sit back in a squat position.

Power jump squats: push off as high as possible.

stabilize the shoulder joint in order for the body to be lowered and raised. Ensure the core muscles are held tight, the legs are kept straight and the movement of the body up and down is slow and controlled. Exhale as you push your body up, and inhale as you return back to the start position. Perform two to three sets of twelve to twenty push-ups, alternating sides after each set.

BELOW LEFT: Off-set push-up..
BELOW RIGHT: Off-set push-up: focus on a tight core and balance.

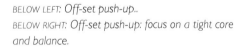

Narrow ball push-up: start with arms extended.

Narrow ball push-up: lower the body slowly.

Narrow Ball Push-Up (advanced)

Place both hands close together on the medicine ball. The body is held in a push-up position. Keep the elbows pointed backward and the abdominal muscles tight as you lower your body toward the floor and push back up. Additional strength in the arms, torso and shoulders is required for this push-up in order to maintain a balanced movement. Using a larger ball gives a larger surface to put the hands on. Perform two to three sets of ten to fifteen push-ups.

Drop Toss Push-Up (advanced) (partner drill)

In a kneeling position hold the ball close to the chest. Toss the ball to your partner and fall forward keeping your body erect. Drop your hands to the floor and perform a push-up immediately. Push back in an explosive motion up to the kneeling position. Your partner tosses the ball back and you repeat the ball toss and push-up. Perform two to three sets of eight to twelve repetitions with a 3–4kg (6–8lb) medicine ball.

Drop toss push-up: toss the ball to your partner.

Drop toss push-up: perform a push-up.

Drop toss push-up: resume kneeling position to receive ball.

Punch Throws (partner drill)

This exercise builds upper body strength and explosive power. Using the same motion as throwing a punch, propel the ball toward your partner. Ensure your core is held tight and the body stays balanced.

BELOW LEFT: Punch throw: straight right.
BELOW RIGHT: Punch throw: execute the straight right.

Punch throw: left jab.

Punch throw: execute the left jab.

Straight right

Start in the boxing stance and hold the ball in your right hand at shoulder level. Throw the ball to your partner. As you extend your arm, rotate your hips, pushing off the back foot in a similar motion to throwing a straight right. Your partner catches the ball and tosses it back to you. Repeat the throw.

Jab

Start in the boxing stance and hold the ball in your left hand at shoulder level. Throw the ball to your partner, focusing on a straight throwing motion. Your partner catches the ball and tosses it back to you. Repeat the throw. Make sure you have sufficient room to do this drill and your partner is ready to receive the throw.

This drill should only be performed using straight lefts and straight rights. Perform two to three sets of fifteen to twenty repetitions for each arm with a 3–4kg (6–8lb) medicine ball.

Full Body Drill

Medicine Ball Slam (advanced)

Place a heavy bag on its side on the floor. Put a medicine ball next to it. Perform a burpee (squat thrust) by starting in a standing position and then dropping into a squat position and placing both hands on the ball. Extend the legs back in a quick motion. Return to the squat position and jump up, raising the medicine ball above your head. Slam it down into the heavy bag, as hard as you can. This is one repetition. If no heavy bag is available, use a thick mat to throw the ball on to. This is a great drill to build upper body endurance, core strength and explosive leg power. The slam works the arms and the shoulders. The burpee works the legs. Perform three sets of ten to twelve repetitions with a 4–5kg (8–10lb) medicine ball.

Medicine ball slam: medicine ball beside heavy bag.

Medicine ball slam: perform a burpee.

LEFT: *Medicine ball slam: get ready to jump.*

BELOW LEFT: *Medicine ball slam: jump high raising the ball overhead.*

BELOW RIGHT: *Medicine ball slam: slam the ball on the heavy bag.*

Medicine ball leg thrust: start position.

Medicine ball leg thrust: pull your legs into one side.

Medicine ball leg thrust: extend the legs.

Medicine ball leg thrust: pull legs into the other side.

Medicine Ball Leg Thrust

Place both hands on the medicine ball so that the body is in a plank position. Pull the legs into the right side of the ball, thrust the legs back into a plank and then pull the legs into a squat position on the left side of the ball. The shoulders and arms must remain stable on the ball as the legs are thrust into the plank position from the side squats. The abdominal muscles are engaged to pull the legs into the side squats. Perform three sets of ten repetitions.

Medicine Ball Punch Drill (partner drill)

One partner holds a large medicine ball securely against the chest with one arm over the top of the ball and the other arm under the ball. The other partner wears boxing gloves, moves around and punches at the medicine ball. The puncher focuses on smoothly moving into range and landing quick strikes, with the emphasis on speed, not power. It is preferable to use a large leather medicine ball for this drill, as they have more give to them. Perform for one three-minute round.

*Medicine ball punch drill:
keep the punches light.*

Core Exercises without the Medicine Ball

A strong core helps to stabilize the back, hips and shoulders, and creates a solid base of support for execution of powerful punches. Here are five basic core strengthening exercises which are performed without the medicine ball.

BELOW LEFT: Abdominal crunch: start.
BELOW RIGHT: Abdominal crunch: raise shoulder blades off the floor.

Abdominal Crunch

The abdominal crunch is the most basic of abdominal exercises. It is similar to a sit-up, but only the upper back is lifted off the floor. If you experience back pain this is a safer abdominal exercise to start with, since the spine is not compromised. Start in a sit-up position, feet on the floor and the hands beside the head. Curl up slowly, lifting only the head and both shoulder blades off the floor. Hold for a two-second count. Keep the lower back against the floor. Repeat in a smooth, controlled motion. Perform three sets of twenty to thirty repetitions.

Twisting Crunch

Start in a sit-up position, hands beside the head. Curl up slowly, lifting the head and one shoulder blade off the floor, rotating through the core and angling off to the left. Lower back to the floor and slowly lift the head and the other shoulder blade off the floor, angling to the right. Repeat. The twisting crunch primarily works the oblique abdominal muscles and the upper portion of the abdominal muscles. Perform two sets of twenty to thirty repetitions.

Twisting crunch: raise one shoulder blade off the floor.

Boxer's Ab Press

Start sitting on the floor and hold your hands in an on-guard position. Pull the knees in toward the chest. Slowly press both legs out in front, allowing the body to move backward slightly. Pause and then slowly return the knees back to the chest. For an easier version, place your hands on the ground behind the body, fingertips facing forward and the elbows slightly bent. Perform three sets of fifteen repetitions.

Boxer's ab press: start with knees pulled in.

Boxer's ab press: extend your legs out.

Boxer's ab press: alternate version, lean back on hands.

Boxer's ab press: alternate version, extend your legs out.

Body plank.

Body plank: leg lifted.

Body Plank

Start from a push-up position on the floor. Bend your elbows at ninety degrees with your body weight on your forearms. Keep your head in line with your back, elbows directly below your shoulders, and body flat. Pull the abdominal muscles up toward the spine. Perform three sets, holding for thirty seconds for each set and working up to sixty seconds for each set. To increase difficulty lift one leg in the air, keeping the leg level with the back foot flexed and core held tight. Hold and then lift the other leg.

Supine Cycle

Start in a sit-up position, hands beside the head and the elbows back. As you bring the left knee toward the chest, rotate the trunk to the left and try to touch the right elbow to the left thigh. At the same time extend the right leg above the floor. Now bring the right knee toward the chest, rotating the trunk to the right and trying to touch the left elbow to the right thigh. This counts as one repetition. Extend the left leg long above the floor. The motion is slow, controlled and continuous, and very much like pedalling a bicycle. Perform two to three sets of twenty to thirty repetitions.

Supine cycle: start.

Supine cycle: finish.

CHAPTER 8

BOXING TRAINING ROUTINES

To be serious about boxing, every element of your training has to be as real as possible and emulate the challenges you are likely to face in the ring. It takes time to attain an elite physical conditioning level and commitment to adhere to a training regimen. The fundamentals of muscular strength, cardiovascular endurance, flexibility, agility, balance and mobility must be acknowledged and built into your training programme.

The Training Effect

Form follows function, and the body will always try to adapt to the demands placed on it. The training effect is the direct result of placing greater demands on the cardiovascular system and musculature system than the body is accustomed to. Properly executing a movement over and over will train the muscles to produce the desired outcome, improving responsiveness, reaction time and effectiveness. You will become physically stronger, with improved cardio-conditioning, which will lead to a better performance. A highly conditioned athlete will always perform at the most efficient level.

Before beginning any training programme, ensure you are healthy, free from any injuries, chronic health conditions or diseases, and always consult a medical professional. Be realistic about your current level of fitness and physical conditioning. Train smart, be well informed and work at a level that will challenge you, but not injure you.

Remember that there are two levels of training a fighter: mastering the technical skills and developing elite physical conditioning. Both go hand in hand.

Train like a Champion

Champions arrive at training camp well-conditioned and with a high fitness level. They have continued with a workout regimen between camps and have an active, clean lifestyle. An average training camp lasts eight to twelve weeks and in some cases the boxers have both a boxing trainer and a strength/conditioning trainer. Training is specifically designed to enhance the boxer's individual strengths and improve upon their weaknesses. A game plan is developed and implemented for dealing with their opponent's style of boxing.

Two workouts are described below. Your current conditioning level will determine which one you use. Boxing training routine 1 gives details on training when starting your boxing journey, and is a great way to stay in fighting shape. Boxing training routine 2 is a more advanced workout that incorporates two workouts in one day. It is also known as a split-style of training.

Pacquiao – always in top shape.

Boxing Training Routine 1

Shadowboxing (three 3-min rounds)

Warm up your muscles by shadowboxing. This first round prepares you mentally to hit the different bags and target mitts, reviewing the execution of the punches. If a mirror is available, check out your stance, making sure the fists are held high, the elbows are in to protect the body, and you are in the classic boxing position. Keep the hands up and move around, side-to-side, front and back. Add some body movement and head movement. Now add some jabs and straight punches. Move around as if you are in the ring, not only throwing punches, but also evading them. Stay loose and in control. Before moving onto the next round, slowly take the limbs through a greater range of motion and lengthen out the muscles. The major areas of concern are the shoulder area, hip flexor and legs (see Chapter 6).

Now that you are warmed up, it is time to get serious and execute the punches with more intent. As with the warm-up, move around, mix up the punches, and keep the heart rate elevated. Working in three-minute rounds, with a one-minute rest in between, devise a game plan of the punches and punch combinations you want to tackle. Develop both offensive moves and defensive moves. This is when you need to be creative. Also work on transitions that do not feel comfortable and smooth. During shadowboxing, you can develop and correct your punching technique, balance and weight transfers from foot to foot, and combinations. Get a feel for the three-minute time limit and pace yourself so you are working at about seventy to eighty per cent of your maximum effort. During the one-minute rest, take time to prepare for the next three-minute round. Ask yourself what punches felt smooth and under control, and what movements did not flow well. Then develop a strategy for improvement.

Jump rope (12min)

Keep the footwork basic and the intensity moderate for about two minutes. Increase the intensity slightly by either performing more intricate footwork or by increasing the speed at which you are jumping. If you are a beginner, divide the jumping into four three-minute rounds and build up to one twelve-minute continuous round. If you are a seasoned jumper, you may want to try some sprints (around the six-minute mark), perform high knee jogging for twenty to twenty-five seconds and then bring the intensity back down for sixty seconds. Repeat four to six times. Jump for a total of twelve minutes.

Shadowboxing: focus on proper punching technique.

Jump rope: develops explosive footwork.

Develop speed and accuracy.

This can be accomplished by working up to the time frame, taking a break when needed, or by reducing the intensity until you have built up your stamina. Remember to use the three-step breakdown when trying new moves (see Chapter 5).

Heavy bag (four 3-min rounds)

Pounding the heavy bag is a great source of tension release, a primal therapy of sorts. Not only does it burn calories and tone muscles, it also benefits the psyche. By repeatedly performing a single punch, the movement and execution will become second nature. This will assist the addition of movement and combinations so they flow easily. Work three minutes for all four rounds and rest between each round for one minute, walking around the bag and reducing the heart rate slightly. Regroup and plan your next attack.

Heavy-bag speed sprints

This advanced punching workout on the heavy bag trains and develops punch speed, works the arm and back muscles for power and endurance, and challenges the cardio-respiratory system. Start with twenty-second sprints, working up to thirty-second sprints. Rest the same amount of time as you work. Walk around and think about your next sprint. Repeat three to four more times. (For more sprint options refer to Chapter 3.)

Focus mitts (three 3-min rounds)

Concentrate on the execution of the punches, working for three three-minute rounds, catching one round then punching one round with your partner. Pay attention to speed, technique and proper execution (see Chapter 4).

Ladder drills on the heavy bag (optional)

If you do not have a partner to work with on the mitts, perform ladder drills on the heavy bag with the left jab, straight right and one-twos (see Chapter 3).

Double-end bag (one 3-min round)

Perform one three-minute round on the double-end bag. Practise your slips and footwork, and mix up your punches (see Chapter 3).

Speed bag (two 3-min rounds)

Incorporating the speed bag into your training will improve coordination and timing. Aim to develop a

Double-end bag.

Build arm endurance.

consistent rhythm when hitting the speed bag, stay focused and do not give up. After workouts with the heavy bag and target mitts, your shoulders will be tired. By finishing your boxing training with speed-bag rounds you will improve shoulder muscle endurance, which helps you keep your hands up.

Cool-down round

The purpose of the cool-down is to decrease the heart rate and review the punches. End with shadowboxing for three to six minutes, punching with light intent, rather than focusing on power. Stay light on your feet, shrugging and rotating the shoulders. Let the muscles relax.

BOXING TRAINING ROUTINE 1: SUMMARY

Shadowboxing (three 3-min rounds)
Round 1   Warm-up shadowboxing. Shadowbox, practising the basic punches and focus on technique and execution. Perform light stretching afterward.
Round 2   Add more intent to your punches.
Round 3   Work at 70–80 per cent of your maximum output. Add offensive and defensive combinations.

Jump Rope (12min)
Jump at a moderate pace for two minutes, increase the pace, mix up the tempo and add a variety of footwork (see Chapter 5).

Heavy Bag (four 3-min rounds)
Choose from the beginner, intermediate or advanced training level. Punch on the heavy bag for three minutes and rest for one minute in between. Perform three rounds (see Chapter 3).

Heavy-Bag Speed Sprints
Start with twenty-second sprints, working up to thirty-second sprints. Rest the same amount of time as you work. Walk around and think about your next sprint. Repeat three to four more times.
Sprint 1   20 seconds (rest 20 seconds)
Sprint 2   20 seconds (rest 20 seconds)
Sprint 3   20 seconds (rest 20 seconds)

Focus Mitts (three 3-min rounds)
Work at your training level: beginner, intermediate or advanced. With a partner alternate three-minute rounds, catching and parrying (see Chapter 4).

Ladder Drills on the Heavy Bag (optional)
Ladder drills can be performed on the heavy bag if you do not have a partner to work with on mitts. Complete twelve punches, working down to one for each jab, straight right and one-two (see Chapter 3).

Double-End bag (one 3-min round)
Focus on single punches, working up to combinations, slipping and practising footwork (see Chapter 3).

Speed Bag (two 3-min rounds)
Work one hand then the other, using single punches and alternating the hands (see Chapter 3).

Cool-Down Round (3–6min)
Shadowboxing will reduce your heart rate and allow you to review your punches

Abdominal Workout (5–8min)
Sample sequence: thirty abdominal crunches then thirty oblique crunches; repeat three times. Fifty to 100 supine cycles, three sets of fifteen abdominal leg presses. Body plank for forty-five to ninety seconds, three sets of twenty hip crunches (see Chapter 7).

Stretches (5–7min)
Always spend time stretching out the muscles and joint areas (see Chapter 6).

Abdominal workout (5–8min)

Now that you have cooled down and your heart rate has decreased, perform abdominal exercises as described in Chapter 7. Concentrate on a controlled execution of the exercises, contracting the abdominal muscles and focusing on the body core muscles. Mix up your choice of abdominal exercises, working for a total of six to ten minutes (see Chapter 7).

Stretches

After each workout, perform stretching and flexibility exercises. This will help lengthen the muscle fibres and reduce soreness the next day (see Chapter 6).

Boxing Training Routine 2 (split routine)

The world's greatest athletes know the importance of being in top cardiovascular condition. For boxers it can mean the difference between 'going the distance' and fading out in the early rounds. The best way to get into fighting shape is to employ a split system of training. This type of training includes an early morning workout and a second workout later in the day.

Morning training session
Roadwork

A day in the life of a fighter starts with an early wake-up, followed by a morning session of running. A five- to ten-minute warm-up is followed by a roadwork session of 6–10km (4–6 miles). Sprints and hill runs are included in the roadwork training three to four times per week in order to replicate the demand for energy during a fight.

Finish the morning session with a cool-down and stretch. Rest well and eat healthily before your next workout (see Chapter 6).

Afternoon training session
Boxing Gym

Later in the day the boxer heads to the gym for several hours for an individual training session. The boxer's routine starts with a thorough warm-up, stretches and shadowboxing. Jump rope is included to perfect the footwork and condition the cardiovascular system. Gruelling bag work and focus mitt work are performed for multiple rounds. Supervised

Roadwork will help you 'go the distance'.

Prepare for your second training session.

sparring sessions are factored into the workout as training progresses. Work on combinations that are specific to the fighting style of your next opponent.

Warm-Up Round (3min)

Warm up your muscles and cardio system by shadowboxing. Perform the basic punches and focus on the technique and the execution. Follow up with light stretches, taking the limbs through the full range of motion.

Shadowboxing (three 3-min rounds)

Now that you are thoroughly warmed up, use 2–3lb hand weights as you shadowbox for the next few rounds.

Warm up for second training session by shadowboxing.

Rounds 1 and 2

Focus on proper punching technique and execution. Put combinations together, adding head movement and developing fluidity between the punches and combinations.

Round 3

Finish your final shadowboxing round without hand weights. Your hands should feel fast and light after dropping the hand weights.

Jump rope (12–20min)

This jump rope workout includes interval sessions of jumping at a moderate pace mixed with repeated periods of higher intensity jumping that last fifteen to thirty seconds. Start by jumping at a moderate pace for four to six minutes. Now jump at a higher intensity performing double unders, high knee sprints and crossovers for fifteen to thirty seconds. Go back to jumping rope at a moderate pace for another two to four minutes and then take the pace up again, repeating the higher intensity jumps. Continue with the intervals and finish off with two minutes of easy jump rope.

Heavy bag (five 3-min rounds)

Mix up the punches and work on various combinations for rounds one to four. Work the bag as if you are in the ring and throw 'punches in bunches'. In the final round (round five), perform a 'three-minute sprint and move drill' with a five-second speed sprint, and then move around the bag for ten seconds. Repeat these intervals for the total three-minute round (see Chapter 3).

Training with a Partner Option

Focus mitts (three 3-min rounds)

If you are training with a partner, alternate between catching and punching. If training without a partner, complete the three three-minute rounds.

Rounds 1 and 2

Start with basic combinations, working up to more complicated drills. Focus on proper technique and execution.

Round 3

Work on complex combinations, at a quick pace, including slipping and footwork (see Chapter 4).

Focus mitt speed drills

Aim for speed, not power, and deliver a series of fast punch sprints. Start with one-twos (straight lefts and rights), for thirty seconds, immediately followed by hooks for thirty seconds, and then uppercuts for thirty seconds. Always maintain proper form and execution. Repeat the drill twice before switching partners.

Sharpen your punches.

Challenge your upper body endurance.

Throw punches from multiple angles.

Training without a Partner Option

If you do not have a partner to work with on the mitts, perform the following drills and sprints on the heavy bag.

Ladder drill on the heavy bag
Perform drills with the left jab, the straight right and then one-twos. Start with twelve jabs as fast as you can, move around for a few seconds and repeat down to one repetition (see Chapter 3).

Heavy bag speed drills
Addressing the heavy bag straight on, check your arm reach and relax the legs. Sprint and rest the same amount of time.

Sprint 1   40 seconds (rest 40 seconds)
Sprint 2   40 seconds (rest 40 seconds)
Sprint 3   30 seconds (rest 30 seconds)
Sprint 4   30 seconds (rest 30 seconds)
Sprint 5   20 seconds (rest 20 seconds)
Sprint 6   20 seconds (rest 20 seconds)

Speed bag (6–9min)
Hit the bag as fast you can, striking with both hands and maintaining control of the bag (see Chapter 3).

Double-end bag (two 3-min rounds)
Include rapid-succession punching, combinations and defensive moves (see Chapter 3).

Cool-down round (one 3-min round)
Shadowbox for three minutes, moving around and throwing lightly.

Abdominal workout
Muscle Conditioning. Sample sequence: abdominal crunches – thirty reps, medicine ball basic curl ups – thirty reps, supine cycle – thirty reps, medicine ball oblique twists – thirty reps, hip raises without medicine ball – thirty reps (see Chapter 7).

Stretches (5–7min)
Always stretch after each workout (see Chapter 6).

Whether you are working out by yourself, or with a partner, or a coach, tailor the workouts for your needs. If your boxing skills and conditioning are at the appropriate level, your coach will factor in sparring sessions.

Drink a sufficient amount of water to stay hydrated before, during and after your training sessions. Choose healthy foods to eat and consume some carbohydrates immediately after your training session. Also, to promote optimal recovery, eat protein-rich foods approximately thirty minutes after your workout. Make time to rest and allow the body to recover.

BOXING TRAINING ROUTINE 2 (SPLIT ROUTINE): SUMMARY

Morning Training Session
Roadwork: 10–14km (6–8 miles)

Boxing Gym Training Session (3–4hr)

Warm-Up Round (3min)
Shadowbox practising the basic punches while focusing on technique and execution. Follow up with light stretches.

Shadowboxing (three 3-min rounds)
Optional: use 2–3lb hand weights.
Rounds 1 and 2   Put combinations together, adding head movement and developing fluidity between the punches and combinations.
Round 3   No weights. Work all the punches together, adding lots of footwork and movement.

Jump Rope (12–20min)
Intervals of moderate-paced skipping mixed with higher intensity sprints. Skip (2–4min), sprint interval (20–30sec; high knees, double jumps, jumping jacks, speed skip), repeat until the last two minutes of this jump rope session, easy skipping (2min) (see Chapter 5).

Heavy Bag (four 3-min rounds)
Work for three minutes and rest for one minute.
Rounds 1–4   Mix up the punches, add footwork and work on combinations. Work the bag as if you are in the ring. Throw the punches in bunches.
Round 5   Burnout drill: five-second speed sprint, move around for fifteeen seconds, repeat for the three-minute round.

OPTION 1: Training with a Partner

Focus Mitts (three 3-min rounds)
Alternate if not training with a coach.

Focus Mitt Speed Drills (One drill per person)

Straight punches	20 seconds
Hooks	20 seconds
Uppercuts	20 seconds

OPTION 2: Training without a Partner

Ladders
Perform drills with left jab, straight right and one-twos (see Chapter 3).

Heavy-Bag Speed Sprints
Face the heavy bag straight on, check your arm reach and relax the legs. Sprint and rest the same amount of time. Repeat twice before switching partners.

Sprint 1	40 seconds (rest 40 seconds)	Sprint 4	30 seconds (rest 30 seconds)
Sprint 2	40 seconds (rest 40 seconds)	Sprint 5	20 seconds (rest 20 seconds)
Sprint 3	30 seconds (rest 30 seconds)	Sprint 6	20 seconds (rest 20 seconds)

Speed Bag (6–9min)
Work on your timing and upper body endurance.

Double-End Bag (two 3-min rounds)
Include rapid-succession punching, combinations and defensive moves (see Chapter 3).

Cool-Down Round (one 3-min round)
Shadowbox for three minutes, moving around and throwing lightly.

Abdominal Workout (6–10min)
Sample sequence: abdominal crunches (three sets of thirty repetitions), medicine ball basic curl-ups (three sets of thirty repetitions), supine cycle (sixty repetitions), medicine ball oblique twists (thirty repetitions), hip raises with medicine ball (thirty repetitions), double V-ups (three sets of ten repetitions) (see Chapter 7).

Stretches (5–7min)
Always stretch after each workout (see Chapter 6).

CHAPTER 9

SPARRING

Boxing requires intense mental focus, a highly developed fitness level, commitment and passion. The muscles and mind work together in a specified synchronism in order to produce an extraordinary outcome. Boxing requires the development of strong, lean muscles. Successful boxers spend thousands of hours in training, practising each movement, repetition after repetition in order to attain precise timing and extreme physical conditioning.

Sparring allows you to throw punches at a live opponent and takes the defensive nature of the sport to another level. Everything that you have practised up to this point is applied under pressure and gives you an opportunity to improve all aspects of your performance. Sparring fine-tunes your skills and simulates fight conditions in a controlled environment. You have to improvise your next move, which make sparring far more complex and intense than punching the heavy bag or focus mitts.

Sparring is not for everyone and should be recognized as a potentially dangerous activity. It should be taken seriously – heavy bags do not strike back

Pacquiao sparring.

but sparring partners do. Before engaging in sparring, you need to be in excellent physical condition. Work on developing the technical and physical skills for a minimum of five to six months. When you are able to go five or six rounds on the heavy bag at a fast pace, run five to six miles including sprints, jump rope for at least fifteen to twenty minutes, and get through a gruelling session on the focus mitts, then you might be ready to spar.

If you have to remind yourself of the basics, such as keeping your hands up, then you will be in trouble the first time you spar. All defensive and offensive moves must be instinctive and automatic. These skills should be honed to a certain degree of proficiency on the focus mitts.

Not only do you require the physical conditioning, the timing and the skill level, it is also necessary to have the correct mind-set.

Only spar under the supervision of an experienced, certified trainer. Follow your trainer's directions. You must wear protective equipment and large sparring gloves (at least 16oz). Spar in a boxing ring or on a cushioned surface, not on a hard floor surface.

Make Intelligent Decisions

Know when you are physically able to spar. Understand how you feel when you are experiencing 'good pain' and are able to push through temporary exhaustion. This is what makes you a better boxer. However, respect if you are injured, experiencing extreme fatigue or excessive muscle pain. Rest may be necessary in order that minor injuries and symptoms do not become chronic. Always keep your trainer informed, make adjustments to your sparring sessions and take the time to recover from an injury or illness.

Directed Sparring

With directed sparring each boxer is given a set of instructions and types of punches to throw. Sessions may include one boxer working on defensive moves (deflecting and slipping punches), and the other working on offensive moves (throwing punches). You

may do one round of sparring just throwing jabs or a session of throwing punches to the body. The trainer may switch roles and will add more elements into the sparring as the instruction continues. Directed sparring allows the boxer to gain confidence before advancing to free-form sparring.

Situational Sparring

Situational sparring develops muscle memory and quick reflexes. It helps to familiarize a boxer with different fighting styles. As you experience sparring with different opponents and in different situations you will start to develop your own fighting style.

Free-Form Sparring

Free-form sparring, also known as open sparring, is the most advanced form of sparring and is performed less frequently (two to three times per week). All aspects of offensive and defensive moves are incorporated into this training and your responses are continually changing. Only spar the number of rounds that you are able to maintain proper form and technique. Spar shorter rounds until you build up your endurance, working your way up to full three-minute rounds. Increase the number of rounds as your conditioning improves. Spar one to two more rounds than the number of rounds you would compete, in order to build physical and mental ring conditioning. Incorporate round robin sparring (sparring one to two rounds with a one round break in between) into your sessions, allowing for training and developing the technical aspects of your performance. Add an additional challenge to your training by shortening the rest intervals between rounds and so decreasing the recovery time.

Sparring is not Fighting!

The goal of a competitive boxing match is to win the contest. Focusing on the quality of your performance, execution and timing are the goals of sparring. The intensity of a sparring session will be influenced by a number of factors and it is necessary for boxers to control their emotions and temper. Due to the competitive nature of the sport, if a novice boxer is sparring with a more experienced boxer, his intensity level may increase due to frustration. By focusing on tactical aspects of the performance during a sparring session, you can learn how to react in a fight situation instead of retaliating with an emotional response.

What to Expect the First Time you Spar

Depending on your boxing experience, your sparring partner's skill level and your trainer's knowledge, your first experience of stepping in the ring may be unnerving. As a novice, your trainer should have you work with an experienced boxer who will not take advantage of your lack of experience. Your trainer will also make sure that you and your sparring partner agree on the pace and intensity of your sparring workout.

New boxers often have difficulty controlling their emotions before a sparring session, due to an increased release of adrenaline in their system, and this could lead to a feeling of nervousness or anxiety. Unlike working the heavy bag, where you can move for four or five rounds and punch when you want

to, you now have a live opponent chasing you and setting the tempo. A feeling of survival in the ring can create a very different scenario than working on the mitts with your trainer. It is difficult to plan under pressure and all the well-practised combinations on the mitts and heavy bag may result in wild swinging punches. Missing your target expends more energy than landing a punch. You are also concentrating on both throwing punches and evading punches.

Emotions must be kept under control, focusing on the task at hand and being in the moment. Sparring is a training session and there are no winners or losers. If winning becomes a goal, then emotions may influence the result.

Positive Visualization

Successful boxers use positive visualization techniques prior to training and during competition. Positive visualization helps to build confidence and improves your ability to perform under pressure and in a variety of situations. Create a mental image of how you want to perform. You may imagine details of a previous best performance, the way it felt and played out. See yourself throwing strong, crisp punches, moving smoothly around the ring, slipping and coming back with a counterpunch.

Focus on tactical aspects of your performance.

Always wear protective equipment in the ring.

As Sergio Martinez relates,

Everything we do is so we train the body and the mind to have balance, so I can respond automatically in a fraction of a second, so that my body knows how to act in this tiny little moment. What must be trained is the mind.

Positive visualization, just like warming up or putting on your hand wraps, needs to be part of your training ritual.

Sparring Gear

Mouth Guard

Never spar without a mouthpiece. A good mouthpiece helps prevent cuts inside the mouth, damage to the teeth and supports the jaw. The mouthpiece should fit comfortably, as it is important to keep your mouth closed. Gel guards, which mould to your teeth, give a good fit. Remember that the gel guard has to be boiled and allowed to mould to your teeth before sparring. The best fit is a dentist-made mouthpiece.

Protective Cups

These protect the groin, hips and kidneys from low blows.

Chest Protector

For females this protects the chest region from punches.

Shoes

Boxing shoes have very little arch support and little padding. They allow you to feel the canvas of the

Boxing shoes allow for quick footwork and easy pivoting.

ring floor, and aid quick footwork and easy pivoting. Only use boxing shoes in the ring or while jumping rope on a wood-sprung floor. For everyday training, if the floor is not cushioned or hard wood, wear a cross-trainer shoe. Save your joints and muscles and keep your boxing shoes for the ring.

Protective Headgear

Headgear is available in different styles and sizes, each providing different levels of protection. The best models offer extra protection without compromising your vision. Make sure the headgear fits snugly, and does not slide around or obstruct your vision.

Hand Wraps

Even if you are wearing the best punching gloves available, you need to ensure your hands are wrapped effectively for protection. No boxing glove on its own can provide sufficient protection for your hands. Effective hand wrapping is essential to give your hands complete protection.

Sparring Gloves

These gloves are made with extra shock-absorbing foam and are at least 16oz in size, since you will be striking an opponent rather than a heavy bag. They are available in either a laced-up or Velcro-fastened version. Make sure the gloves are in good condition with no tears or cracks in the leather and check inside them to ensure that the foam and protective padding is not breaking up. Only use these gloves for sparring, not bag work or focus mitt work.

Defensive Moves

The number one rule in boxing is 'protect yourself at all times'. There is a constant shift between offensive and defensive movement when sparring. Before launching an offensive attack you must first learn to protect yourself.

Always wear your headgear when sparring.

Wear sparring gloves that are in good condition.

Protect yourself at all times.

Keep Your Hands Up

The arms and gloves act as a basic shield to defend the body and head. The boxing basics need to be reviewed again. The arms are kept close to the sides of the body to protect the rib cage and solar plexus, and the fist/gloves up by the face and chin to protect the head (see Chapter 2).

Head Movement

Constant head movement can disrupt your opponent's rhythm and allows you to slip your opponent's punches. This leaves your hands free to counter-punch. Always keep your hands up in the protective position and do not make the mistake of dropping your hands when moving your head.

Head movement.

Blocking a left hook to the head.

Blocking a right hook to the head.

Blocking a left hook to the body.

Blocking a right hook to the body.

Blocking

The most fundamental and defensive method is blocking. With your hands up and tight against your head, use the outside portion of the gloves to block headshots. Keep the elbows close to the body and use the elbow or forearm to block body punches. Mickey Ward was an expert at blocking punches. He had to be as he almost never moved his head (see Chapter 4).

Parrying

Parrying a punch involves 'catching' it and then redirecting it aside. The body does not move, only the hand. To parry, turn the palm of your glove to catch the knuckles of your opponent's glove. Keep your glove at your chin and wait for the punch to come to you. Do not reach or paw for the punch. Protect yourself by keeping your arms and elbows close to the torso (see Chapter 4).

Parrying works best against straight punches. Parry with the right hand against the opponent's left jab. This leaves your left hand free to follow up with your own jab. Your left hand defends against your opponent's incoming right, giving an opportunity for a counterpunch. Once you are confident with parrying, you can manipulate it by defecting and redirecting your opponent's glove down, either to the inside or outside. Timing the parry is crucial as you leave yourself open if you do not redirect the oncoming punch at the right moment. You can use parries to

Parry a left jab.

Parry a straight right.

defend against uppercuts. Use the opposite hand to parry the incoming uppercut. This is a risky move and it is better to avoid the uppercut by stepping back and counterpunching. In their prime, Oscar De La Hoya and Evander Holyfield were great at parrying punches.

Use your left glove to parry a right uppercut.

Use your right glove to parry a left uppercut.

Ducking under a left hook.

Ducking a left jab and countering with a body shot.

Ducking

Ducking refers to moving the head and body beneath an incoming punch. Move the head underneath the incoming punch, bending at your knees quickly and keeping your eyes on your opponent. For straight punches move down quickly and return quickly to the on-guard position. To slip a hook, as you duck down, shift your body weight slightly to the left or right. Once you have dodged the punch, return quickly to your boxing stance. Ducking expends a great deal of energy and requires excellent timing. It works well against sluggers that like to throw big looping hooks. To become comfortable and effective with ducking, work with your coach using target mitt drills. Boxers who were masters at ducking punches, or 'bobbing and weaving', were Jack Dempsey, Rocky Marciano, Joe Frazier and Mike Tyson.

Slipping

Slipping is an effective defensive technique and gets you out of the way of an oncoming punch and at the same time keeps you in the range to counterpunch. Instead of blocking an oncoming punch, slipping can be used by utilizing a side-to-side movement of the head and shoulders and bending the knees so that the oncoming punch 'slips' safely past you. The body stays directly over the legs, slightly forward and not leaning back.

Slipping an oncoming punch is an art and can put your opponent at a disadvantage. It effectively frees up your arms to counterpunch. Choosing the right moment to slip is critical. The timing and confidence to utilize this advanced defensive move needs to be practised during shadowboxing, target mitt drills and controlled sparring. Excessive slipping wastes energy.

One of the greatest defensive fighters of all times is Floyd Mayweather Jr. With his incredible speed and timing he avoids his opponent's punches with ease. He is a master of the art of slipping (see Chapter 4).

Basic Slips

Slipping the left jab
Hands up, knees bent. Move your head and shoulders to the right just enough to clear the jab.

Counterpunch option   Slip and counter with a jab to the head or body.

Slipping a left jab.

Slipping a straight right.

After slipping a jab counter with a right to the head or body.

Slipping the right hand

With your hands up, bend your knees slightly, slip to the left to avoid the right hand.

Counterpunch option   Return with a left hook to the body or left hook to the head.

Slipping Tips

- The whole point of slipping is to avoid a punch and create an opening for a counterpunch.
- Slipping keeps your arms free so you can counterpunch.
- If you have avoided a punch by slipping, that is a good thing, but you do not want to continually use slipping just to avoid punches. It is a waste of energy and opportunity.
- If you are not going to counterpunch, then you are better off blocking or parrying the punch.
- If you continually slip without responding with a counterpunch, your opponent will recognize that you are not going to throw a punch, learn your slipping pattern and retaliate.

Successful boxers use defensive moves to avoid punches and at the same time set up their own attacks. When you block or slip or parry a punch, come out of that defensive move with a counterpunch. The more you spar the more you will become aware of your opponent's counterpunches. For example, when you throw a jab you may expect a right cross from your opponent. Work on target mitt counterpunch drills with your coach to develop natural defensive reflexes.

Fundamental defensive tips

- Never take your eyes off your opponent.
- Keep your hands up and chin down.
- Keep moving.
- Get back on balance quickly.
- Do not lean back to avoid punches.
- Stay out of the corners.
- Stay off the ropes.
- Move your head or your opponent will move it for you.

Offensive Moves

Movement

Effective movement is an offensive tool as well as an essential defensive method. Fluid movement is essential in the ring, and therefore it is important that movement be well practised in the gym.

Find your range.

Southpaw Chad Dawson uses crisp jabs to set up his attack.

Focus on clean, effective punches.

Range

Range is the amount of distance between you and your opponent. The use of effective range will allow you to hit your opponent while giving you the time to manoeuvre defensively.

Jab, Jab, Jab!

As the most frequently thrown punch, the main purpose of the jab is to keep your opponent off-guard and at a safe distance. It sets up more powerful punches, keeps your opponent off-balance and can be used to dictate the pace of the fight. The jab is the fastest and safest punch in your arsenal. Start off your offence with crisp, clean jabs. For Muhammad Ali, Larry Holmes and Sugar Ray Leonard the jab was the key to their success.

Clean Punches

In amateur boxing a clean punch must land directly with the knuckle portion of the closed glove. The punches must land above the belt of the opponent and in front or at the sides of the head or body. A 'slapping punch' or making contact with the palm side of the glove is a common mistake and must be avoided.

Combinations

Do not get comfortable with throwing just jabs. If you can catch your opponent with your jab, it is time to add combinations and keep him off-guard. Start to throw one-twos (jab-cross) and put more power into your punches. Sometimes you can pierce your opponent's defence on the first punch, sometimes it opens up on the second or third punch. Keep throwing combinations to take advantage of all opportunities. Stay busy (see Chapter 3).

Feints

Feints create opportunities to off-set your opponent's rhythm. By drawing your opponent into responding to the feint, you are able to produce an opportunity for a counterpunch. The incomplete attacks of feinting, such as slightly moving your shoulders, fists, feet or body will cause a reaction from your opponent. Two examples of feints are: (1) feint a jab to the body, so your opponent will drop their guard and quickly throw a jab to the head; (2) feint with your feet by quickly moving the feet a half-step to the left and then moving them to the right, possibly creating an opening and an opportunity (see Chapter 2).

Counterpunching

Counterpunching is the most important offensive skill to learn. There is only a small opportunity to respond with a counterpunch while your opponent is throwing a punch at you. You have to think about both protecting yourself and at the same time landing your own effective punch. With practice more creative counters can be learned.

The benefits of counterpunching
• The best time to hit your opponent is when he is throwing a punch.
• Counterpunches stop your opponent's momentum.
• Counterpunches will make your opponent cautious.
• The only way to go from defence to offence is to counterpunch.

Examples of possible counterpunches
When your opponent throws a jab:

• Parry with your right glove and throw a counter jab straight back into the head. Keep the jab shoulder high and chin tucked to protect from a one-two (jab–right cross), retaliation.

• Slip to the outside and then throw a jab to the head or the body.
• Duck, bend your knees, lowering your body and throw a counter jab straight to your opponent's solar plexus.
• Duck and jab and throw a cross to the body.

When your opponent throws a jab to the body:

• Block the punch with the lead elbow and come back with a right cross to the head.
• Take a half-step back to avoid the punch and quickly move forward with a quick hook to the head.

When your opponent throws a lead right:

• Block with your left glove as you roll with the punch.
• Immediately come back with your own right cross.
• Catch/parry the incoming right with your left glove.
• Throw a quick straight right to the head.
• Slip to the outside and throw a left hook to the body.
• Slip to the outside and throw a straight right to the head or body.

When your opponent throws a right lead to the body:

• Block with the elbow and throw a straight right to the head.
• Take a half-step back.
• Quickly move forward and throw a left uppercut to the head.

When your opponent throws a hook:

• Block the punch and come back with a straight one-two combination.
• Duck under the hook and come back with a one-two to the body.
• Take a half-step back to avoid the hook.
• Come back with a straight counterpunch and then a quick jab to the head.

When your opponent throws a hook to the body:

- Block the punch with your elbow.
- With your free hand counter with a hook to the head or the body.
- Take a half-step back and throw a jab to the head.

When your opponent throws an uppercut:

- If your opponent telegraphs (winds up) the uppercut, throw a quick jab or one-two to the head.
- Catch the uppercut and throw a quick uppercut to the head.

Remember to move your head and body after throwing combinations. Constantly give your opponent angles. Never stand in front of them for too long, allowing them to get set. Practise counterpunching drills at three-quarter speed with a partner. These sessions should always be supervised by a coach.

Fundamental offensive tips
- Move and jab.
- Don't hesitate with your counterpunches.
- Counterpunch in combinations.

- Do not be predictable.
- Mix up your combinations.
- Feint punches.
- Throw punches to the body.
- Work harder than your opponent.

Boxing Different Styles

Take every opportunity to spar with different opponents. The more experience you have of sparring against a variety of styles, the better your understanding of how to fight your opponents. Stay focused even when you get hit. Shake it off. Successful boxers maintain focus even when they get hit.

Sparring with a Tall Boxer

A taller opponent has a reach advantage and will expect you to try to get inside to land your punches. Never underestimate your opponent, whatever their size, apparent speed or strength.

Tactics
- Be busier and throw two to three punches to get inside.
- Work the body once you get inside, making your

Spar against boxers with a variety of fighting styles.

opponent drop his arms to protect his body and creating an opportunity for head punches.

- Utilize slipping and moving from side to side, making your opponent look for you.
- Move to your opponent's jab side, away from the strong straight punches.
- Throw in feints, mix up your punches and be unpredictable.

Sparring with a Shorter Boxer

When you spar against a shorter opponent they will try to get inside to work the body, throwing shorter punches, and will duck under your punches. This will take away your reach advantage.

Tactics
- Work your jab and keep your distance, preventing your opponent from getting inside.
- Snap your punches, keeping your opponent on the end of your punches.
- Be active, move around using the entire ring, making your opponent move and expend energy.
- Keep your chin tucked in.

Sparring with a Wild Boxer

Wild boxers are often inexperienced and scared. Their punches are unpredictable and you do not want to get caught with a lucky punch.

Tactics
- Stay true to your style of fighting and your game plan.
- Maintain proper form, so you do not leave yourself open to lucky shots.
- Be ready for the wild boxer to take lunging steps as they move forward.
- Sidestep, duck, step backward to keep them off-guard.
- Wild boxers tend to throw looping, wide punches. Take advantage of this and throw straight punches down the middle.
- Mix them up with feints.

- Move them backward with numerous jabs, as often they are not comfortable throwing punches when they are moving backward.

Sparring with a Slugger

Sluggers have a hard, forceful punch and tend to move straight forward to attack their opponent. They often will take two to three shots in order to set up and land their own big punches. Joe Frazier is one of the best examples of this type of fighter. The legendary trilogy of fights between Joe Frazier and Muhammad Ali demonstrates the classic slugger versus slick boxer match-up.

Tactics
- Constantly move, creating lots of angles, so the slugger has less time to get set.
- Move quickly in and out, attacking suddenly and throwing rapid-fire jabs.
- Do not stand toe-to-toe. Stay out of their reach.
- Circle away from the slugger's power side.
- Throw feints to gauge the reaction of your opponent.

Sparring with a 'Slick' Boxer

A perfect example of a slick boxer is Sugar Ray Leonard. 'Slick' boxers have great footwork and like to move a lot. They have a wide range of punches at their disposal, utilizing a variety of angles and defensive tactics.

Tactics
- Be ready to counterpunch. 'Slick' boxers tend to throw multiple jabs, so be prepared to counterpunch.
- Use lots of head movement to offset their jab.
- Mix up how you react to their jab. Parry the jab, slip the jab, or move away.
- Stay in control. 'Slick' boxers wait for you to make a mistake. Be patient, use your jab to create openings and then throw effective combinations.
- Force the action, moving your opponent backward.

Sparring with a Southpaw Boxer

Southpaw is the normal stance for a left-handed boxer. This boxer has his right hand and right foot forward. They lead with right jabs and follow with left crosses and left hooks. Most boxers fight in the orthodox style (right-handed fighter with the left lead) and it can be challenging when sparring against a southpaw (left-handed boxer). Because southpaws have more opportunities to spar with orthodox fighters, the southpaw has a greater advantage.

Great southpaw boxers include Marvelous Marvin Hagler, Antonio Tarver, Manny Pacquiao and Sergio Martinez. The great rivalry between Juan Manuel Márquez and Manny Pacquiao is a classic example of an orthodox fighter versus a southpaw fighter.

Tactics

- When a southpaw throws a right jab parry with your left.
- Counter with your own right hand to the head or body.
- Throw lead right hands.
- Circle to your left and lead away from their power punch.
- Feint with a right and come back with a left hook.

Set specific goals for each training session. Prepare yourself by using positive visualization. Be in the best physical shape possible in order to practise your skills and give maximum attention and effort. Effective controlled sparring develops reaction time, improves conditioning and prepares you for fighting in the ring.

COMMON ERRORS AND QUICK FIXES

Error: Signalling your intentions (telegraphing). The fist is pulled back or drops slightly before executing the punch.

Quick fix: Fire crisp clean punches directly from your chin to the target.

Error: Boxer drops one hand while throwing the other.

Quick fix: Dropping your non-punching hand from the on-guard/protective position leaves you vulnerable to counterpunches. Practise in front of a mirror. During focus mitt training your coach can tap you with the focus mitt when you drop your hand as a reminder.

Error: Not throwing enough punches. New boxers often become frustrated if their punches are not landing. There is a tendency to stop throwing punches, especially if they are getting hit.

Quick fix: You have to throw a punch in order to land a punch. Be aggressive. Combinations create openings.

Error: Becoming frustrated or angry.

Quick fix: There is no place for frustration or anger in sparring. Successful boxers must maintain control at all times. If you cannot handle getting hit or get upset that your punches are not effective, then you are not emotionally ready to spar.

Error: Poor conditioning.

Quick fix: Ensure you have the necessary physical conditioning to spar. Do not waste your time, your sparring partner's time and your coach's time. Be honest with yourself. Put in the necessary hours in the gym before you step into the ring to spar. Train hard, so your performance in the ring can be explosive and intense for the entire training session.

Error: Hesitating with your punches.

Quick fix: A half-thrown punch is worthless. It is a waste of energy and leaves you vulnerable to counterpunches. Commit to your punches and throw them with confidence.

Error: Getting trapped in the corner.

Quick fix: If your opponent has backed you into a corner, disrupt his attack with quick punches of your own, to create an opening. When an opening presents itself, move rapidly to get out of the corner. Your defensive options are limited when caught in a corner.

Error: Flinching, not keeping your eyes open and/or panicking and holding your breath when punches come your way.

Quick fix: One way of breaking the habit of flinching is to practise the 'tapping drill' with your coach or partner. Move forward and backward with your hands held high in the guard position, as light punches are thrown at your gloves in a random manner. Get used to blocking punches, developing a comfortable breathing rhythm and keeping your eyes open.

MENTAL TOUGHNESS

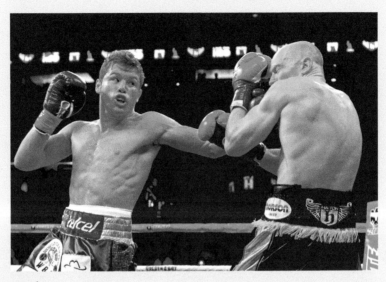

Saúl Álvarez 'El Canelo'.

I was only 12 when my brother Rigoberto made his professional boxing debut. I started to box because of him. I said to him, 'I want to be like you' and he said 'no you will be better'.

My trainer Jose 'Chepo' Reynoso tells me, 'You'll likely become a great champion, but only part of your life. You'll be a person all of your life, so strive to excel at it.'

I keep in mind the need to be humble and have faith in myself. I look back and remember where I came from. What I want is right here and I'm not letting go. You must give your heart and soul in every exercise, in every workout, in every technique and in every fight. With every fight I learn and show advances. I'm improving all the time and I know I still have a lot to learn. There is always room for improvement, and each new fight provides a new challenge.

I keep working hard to achieve my goals. Successful boxers set goals and realize they must pay the price for success. I know all those early morning runs and 100 degree days working in the gym will pay off. Every day an opportunity is presented for me to get better and improve. I will be resilient and not let anything defeat my belief and spirit. I think about winning … that gives me strength to continue. Prepare yourself to be a warrior athlete of character. Never allow any opponent to work harder than you. Never back down.

Mental toughness is aggressiveness under control. It is consistency, focus and tenacity. Mental toughness is the courage to face your fears.

I want to get to the highest point in boxing and I want to be the best that comes out of Mexico. My dream is to be like Muhammad Ali. I want to be like him or even greater.

When people talk about boxing I want them to think about Canelo.

I will leave my heart in the ring to please all the people. I will always bring my fans a great fight and at the end of the day we will yell 'Viva Mexico!'

Saúl Álvarez 'El Canelo'

Saúl Álvarez is the current WBC Light Middleweight Champion. Boxing runs in the Álvarez blood. All seven brothers once fought on the same night. The event was called the 'Álvarez Seven'.

CHAPTER 10

MOTIVATION

MOTIVATION

Julio César Chávez Jr.

I choose to box, not because my father was a great fighter; I choose to box because it's in my blood. My father was such a dominant dynamic fighter. He was the classic, tough, never-give-up Mexican Warrior. For me, it is not about the money, or the fame. It is about the legacy. It is about blunt truth – truth at the end of a fist. In the ring we are all equal.

In Spain they have the running of the bulls. I understand the need to stand all alone in the crowds of those narrow streets and watch my destiny come hurtling towards me, eyes flashing, nostrils flaring. I understand those men as I understand my opponents, as I understand myself.

In boxing there is nothing more important than a positive attitude. The difference between winning and losing is often dictated by a boxer's attitude. A positive attitude allows you to accomplish extraordinary things and achieve your goals.

Motivation is pride, guts, determination and desire. Successful boxers are motivated and dedicated to becoming excellent athletes. They sacrifice and push themselves to reach the next level. It is about finding your inner strength and persevering in pressure situations. This is what leads to success.

People ask me, 'Why did you choose boxing?' I say to them, 'boxing chose me'.

Julio César Chávez Jr

Julio César Chávez Jr is the son of legendary boxing champion Julio César Chávez. He was born when his father was the WBC Junior Lightweight Champion. Julio is the current WBC Middleweight Champion.

Successful Boxers in Action

'A picture says a thousand words.' Here are some images of the world's best boxers in action and a great technical review of the punches.

Jabs

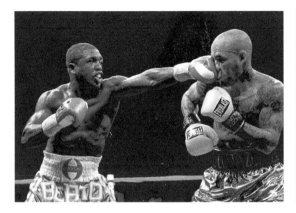

'The ring is a cold place where the truth comes out' says Andre Berto.

A stiff jab will stop your opponent in his tracks.

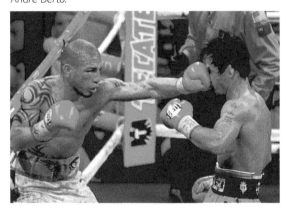

Jabs should be the most frequently thrown punch in your arsenal.

Use jabs to set up power punches.

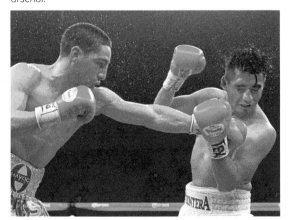

Penetrate your opponent's defenses.

When jabbing, keep right hand on-guard.

Straight Right/Right Cross

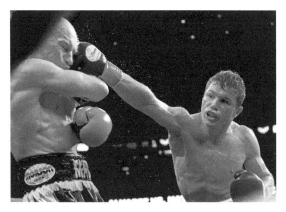

Get your body behind the punch.

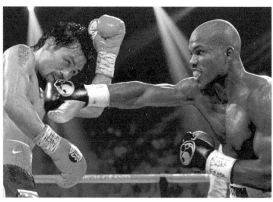

Throw straight to your target.

Follow up with a counterpunch.

Use your jab to set up your right cross.

Pivot on your trail foot for more power.

Throw your power punches with control and stay on-balance.

Hooks

Set up your hooks with quick straight punches.

The most dangerous punch is the one you don't see.

Rotate your body with the hook.

Be ready to follow up.

Throw feints to set up your hooks.

Never stand in front of your opponent too long.

Uppercuts

Don't telegraph your uppercuts.

Keep your opponent on the end of your punches.

Stay focused even if you get hit.

Maintain proper form.

Don't hesitate with your punches.

Work harder than your opponent.

Body Shots

Use body punches to create openings to the head.

Force the action by moving your opponent backward.

Be busier than your opponent.

Throw multiple punches to get inside.

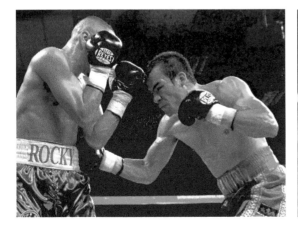

Think 'body and head' when planning your combinations.

Utilize slipping movements to set up a body attack.

151

Counterpunches

The best time to hit your opponent is when he is throwing a punch.

Counterpunches will stop your opponent's momentum.

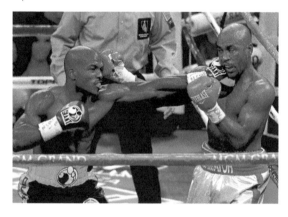

Work your jab and keep your distance, preventing your opponent from getting inside.

Move your head or your opponent will move it for you.

Focus on protecting yourself and at the same time landing your own punches.

Let your hands go and punch with confidence.

AMATEUR AND PROFESSIONAL BOXING

The thrill of being in command of the body, the hard physical toil of withstanding the punches, practising combinations, slipping and throwing punches and the feel of victory are common to both amateur and professional boxing. The conditioning, the functional techniques, and the finesse are alike. The governing bodies and rules are not alike, however, and even though the outcome is the same, a winner and a loser, the fight in the ring is very different.

In England, the Amateur Boxing Association was established in 1880, and in the United States the United States Amateur Boxing Federation (now USA Boxing) was established in 1888. Both were essential in developing the basis for clubs, and promoting safe competition for athletes of all ages and abilities.

In amateur boxing the match is a contest of skill, not brute force, or aggressive power. Fundamentals are stressed, especially defensive moves. The foundation of amateur boxing promotes an effective, fun and safe sport and enforces strict rules to ensure protection. Amateur boxing requires a daily commitment to learning and developing the skills and physical conditioning. Points are awarded for landing clean and effective punches. An amateur boxer's intent is to outbox the opponent by landing clean, effective punches, rather than knocking out the opponent. The boxer with the better technique, more effective punches, better defensive moves, and superior conditioning will be the winner.

Amateur boxing is at the heart of all boxing and is considered the purest form. It is the essence of the sport and is highly regarded as a sport that does not focus on monetary gains. Amateur boxing is used as a vehicle to instruct sportsmanship and the values of physical conditioning. It provides a positive path to release frustrations and energies, and it builds self-confidence and character. The governing body provides certified coaching programs, and arranges respected contests with bouts that are short, well supervised and well refereed; it also acknowledges outstanding, athletic achievements. In 1946 the International Boxing Association (AIBA) was formed, and began to govern Olympic-style amateur boxing for all countries.

Amateur boxing takes more precautions than professional boxing to ensure safety. Protective equipment is mandatory for each competition and the gloves and headgear are required to have exact combinations of a variety of shock-absorbing foams to reduce the impact of a blow.

The Olympic style of boxing is the basis of the sportsmanship of amateur boxing, and many of the great male professionals started in the world of amateur boxing and Olympic glory – men such as Muhammad Ali, Joe Frazier, George Foreman, Evander Holyfield, Sugar Ray Leonard, Lennox Lewis, Floyd Mayweather Jr and Oscar De La Hoya. Amateur boxing often gives the professional boxing arena its next outstanding contestants. It is a great training field to learn, practise and develop into a professional boxer.

In professional boxing a skilful fighter is recognized and celebrated, but often fans want to see a fierce, brutal battle. No headgear is worn and fewer safety precautions are enforced. The boxing gloves do not have the same amount of padding as amateur boxing gloves. The intent is to inflict damage and send your opponent to the canvas as fast as possible.

from *Knockout Fitness* by Andy Dumas and Jamie Dumas

Weight Classes

Weight classes were established in the 1850s, starting with three divisions: lightweight, middleweight and heavyweight. The actual poundage fluctuated within each class, and often caused disputes in championship bouts. In 1909 the National Sporting Club determined fixed poundage for eight classes, and in 1910 nine divisions were set. Today in professional boxing there are seventeen recognized weight divisions for men and eighteen for women, while amateur boxing recognizes only eleven weight classes for men and thirteen for women.

Weight divisions exist in boxing to ensure competitors are evenly matched in size. It simply would not be fair to have a 200lb boxer fight a 140lb boxer. Men's professional, women's professional, and amateur (Olympic) boxing each have their own list of classes and associated weights. The weights and classes in women's professional boxing vary only slightly from those of the men.

Professional Boxing Weight Classes

Division name	Weight
Strawweight/mini-flyweight	up to 47.6kg (105lb)
Junior flyweight	47.6–48.9kg (105–108lb)
Flyweight	48.9–50.8kg (108–112lb)
Super flyweight/junior bantamweight	50.8–52.2kg (112–115lb)
Bantamweight	52.2–53.5kg (115–118lb)
Super bantamweight/junior featherweight	53.5–55.3kg (118–122lb)
Featherweight	55.3–57.2kg (122–126lb)
Super featherweight/junior lightweight	57.2–59.0kg (126–130lb)
Lightweight	59.0–61.2kg (130–135lb)
Super lightweight/junior welterweight	61.2–63.5kg (135–140lb)
Welterweight	63.5–66.7kg (140–147lb)
Super welterweight/junior middleweight	66.7–69.9kg (147–154lb)
Middleweight	69.9–72.6kg (154–160lb)
Super middleweight	72.6–76.2kg (160–168lb)
Light heavyweight	76.2–79.4kg (168–175lb)
Cruiserweight	79.4–90.7kg (175–200lb)
Heavyweight	90.7kg plus (over 200lb)

Amateur (Olympic) Boxing Weight Classes

Division name	Weight (men)	Weight (women)
Light flyweight	46–49kg (101–108lb)	45–48kg (99–106lb)
Flyweight	49–52kg (108–115lb)	48–51kg (106–112lb)
Bantamweight	52–56kg (115–123lb)	51–54kg (112–119lb)
Featherweight		54–57kg (119–126lb)
Lightweight	56–60kg (123–132lb)	57–60kg (126–132lb)
Light welterweight	60–64kg (132–141lb)	60–64kg (132–141lb)
Welterweight	64–69kg (141–152lb)	64–69kg (141–152lb)
Middleweight	69–75kg (152–163lb)	69–75kg (152–163lb)
Light heavyweight	75–81kg (163–178lb)	75–81kg (163–178lb)
Heavyweight	81–91kg (178–201lb)	Unlimited
Super heavyweight	Unlimited	

Pacquioa and Cotto in fighting shape.

Female Boxing

Female boxing became a phenomenon in the 1970s, but there was resistance in the sport to include female fights in the ring. When fights did occur they were considered to be an opening novelty act. The women of this era, however, trained hard, demonstrated high skill levels, and opened up the door for many of today's female boxers.

In 1988 a revival of female boxing took place when the Swedish Boxing Association sanctioned female boxing matches. The British Amateur Boxing Association sanctioned its first boxing competition for women in 1997. USA Boxing eventually agreed to develop a national women's amateur division. There are now more than two thousand registered female boxers in the United States.

During the 1990s, women's professional boxing peaked in popularity with world champions such as Bonnie Canino, Christy Martin, Laila Ali, Licia Rijker and Laura Serrano. The WBC sanctions women's world championship bouts, and fights are held in more than one hundred countries worldwide. According to the Amateur Boxing Association of England, there are nearly one thousand registered female boxers in Britain, up from seventy in 2005.

Jill Diamond of the WBC Female Championship Committee says,

> The WBC was the first of the recognized, non-gender belts given to women. It was a tremendous shot in the arm for women's boxing. With the belt came recognition, better pay and, finally, validation. Outside of the USA, woman's boxing really began to thrive. Within the USA, it was alive and punching, but in my opinion, the culture and, more importantly, the major promoters and TV networks, didn't give it the exposure it needed. And then came the economic crash a couple of years ago. I know from my own experience as head of the Female Championship Committee for the NABF (North American Boxing Federation), and co-Chair for the WBC, women's boxing took a hit.

Laila Ali lands a punch.

No one was taking chances even though we all know that when a good women's fight appears on a card, people go wild.

Things are looking better now, and my hope, like all people who are genuine fans, is that the Olympics will give women's boxing a needed boost. It has already garnered a lot of PR for the women involved, and it will be the first time women's boxing will be seen on national TV. It will bring more women into the gym and possibly encourage more marketing deals for the athletes. I think the future is bright.

In 2009, International Olympic Committee (IOC) president Jacques Rogge announced the inclusion of women's boxing in the 2012 Olympic Games in London. British sports minister Gerry Sutcliffe remarked: 'This move is a massive boost for women's boxing and will help raise the profile of women's boxing at all levels.' Great Britain's Nicola Adams became the first woman in history to receive an Olympic boxing medal, winning a gold medal at the 2012 Olympics. Certainly the sport will benefit from the positive worldwide exposure that the 2012 Olympics provided.

Female boxers are as committed to their craft as their male counterparts. These athletes are disciplined and dedicated to learning the sport and reaching the highest level of boxing ability and expertise.

The Lure of Boxing

The men and women who embrace the challenge of the 'sweet science' are attracted to the thrill of

The lure of boxing.

the sport. As a boxer you are the sum of all of your training. It is the process of learning and perfecting technique, developing self-discipline, self-confidence and inner toughness that will help you become a successful boxer. It requires an inner desire and dedication to build the skill, agility, power and conditioning to compete in this sport.

Russ Anber suggests that,

> Boxing has some kind of evil magnetism about it that draws you to it and yet you find an inner beauty in it and you see the fire and the grace and beauty inside the ring. When a man is trying to do as much damage as he possibly can, we see the elegance of that execution and I think that's what draws people to it and the larger than life heroes that have emerged from the sport.

Boxing started out as a gruesome sport during the ancient Greek and Roman era. It combined the fundamentals of both boxing and wrestling and allowed all sorts of questionable conduct. Biting and kicking were allowed and iron-studded thongs were worn on the hands. Matches were vicious and usually ended when one of the fighters was either seriously injured or dead. The last man standing was the victor. The 668 BC Olympics, held in Athens, Greece, required the boxers to wear protective headgear during the warm-up sessions and leather hand straps for competition. The Greeks appreciated the skill and proficiency required in the sport and supported this forward movement in all the matches held outside the Olympic Games. During the Roman Empire, however, the use of studded hand straps and grisly combat was the expectation and the gladiator style of fighting returned with little importance placed on skill.

In the 1600s matches continued to be a brutal sport with few rules. In the latter part of the century though, the use of only the fists and the skill of punching became the accepted way to box. Matches still were not stopped and there was no restriction on where the punches could be thrown. In 1723 the first boxing ring to be built in England was commissioned by King George I, in Hyde Park, London. At this time boxing was increasing in popularity and was being supported by fencing clubs. It was recognized that the footwork and arm movement skills of a fencer would work well in the ring.

In the 1700s, British fighter James Broughton developed the first set of official rules for boxing, known as the Broughton Rules of 1743. Broughton believed that vicious attacks and death should not be included in the sport of boxing after his opponent died at the end of their fight. Fighting establishments and boxers endorsed these rules for nearly one hundred years. They included: no hitting and grabbing below the waist, the use of boxing gloves during sparring practice, no hitting a person on the ground, and discontinuation of the fight if a fighter knelt down, was on the ground or badly injured. Umpires watched for fair play and sportsmanship in the ring.

In 1867 the Marquess of Queensberry rules were adopted. A time limit of three minutes for each round was set, with a one-minute rest in between. Boxing matches, however, could still go up to forty-five rounds and last over two hours. The maximum number of rounds was reduced to twenty and then fifteen rounds for a championship match, with the maximum of twelve rounds established in the late 1980s. This is the current worldwide maximum number of rounds.

Characteristics of a Successful Boxer

> Discipline, dedication, good physical conditioning, humility to learn, a valiant heart, fists of steel and a winning mental attitude, are the characteristics of a successful boxer.
>
> *José Sulaimán, WBC President*

A successful boxer:

- has a positive attitude towards boxing training
- follows direction from the coach
- stays focused during training
- completes roadwork at least three times per week
- feels confident before a sparring session
- has the ability to respond to an opponent's style quickly

- uses the entire ring
- has the ability to deliver punches with speed and accuracy
- stays off the ropes and out of corners
- shows good use of defensive moves to avoid punches
- has the ability to adapt and learn new skills
- shows respect: shakes hands with opponent after sparring or after competition.

Final Thoughts

When training, give it your all. Prepare as though you are training for the championship of the world. Work the fundamentals and develop the physical conditioning, agility and style. Only then will you be ready to test your skills in the ring. The sweat equity that you put into your sport, the early morning runs, sparring sessions, focus mitt drills and bag work will demonstrate your true passion for boxing. A book is a starting point for inspiration and knowledge. We hope this book inspires you to take pride in your performance. Enjoy your journey.

Sportsmanship.

RIGHT: *Train like a champion.*
BELOW: *Champions stay focused during training.*

INDEX